Sophronia Maria Elliott

The chemistry of cooking and cleaning

Sophronia Maria Elliott

The chemistry of cooking and cleaning

ISBN/EAN: 9783744786010

Printed in Europe, USA, Canada, Australia, Japan

Cover: Foto ©Lupo / pixelio.de

More available books at **www.hansebooks.com**

THE CHEMISTRY

OF

COOKING AND CLEANING

A MANUAL FOR HOUSEKEEPERS

BY

ELLEN H. RICHARDS

AND

S. MARIA ELLIOTT

Second Edition

Revised and Rewritten.

BOSTON
HOME SCIENCE PUBLISHING CO.
1897

First Edition.
Copyright, 1881.
By Estes & Lauriat.

Second Edition.
Copyright, 1897.
By Home Science Publishing Co.

PREFACE.

IN this age of applied science, every opportunity of benefiting the household should be seized upon.

The family is the heart of the country's life, and every philanthropist or social scientist must begin at that point. Whatever, then, will enlighten the mind, and lighten the burden of care, of every housekeeper will be a boon.

At the present time, when the electric light and the gas stove are familiar topics, there is, after all, no branch of science which might be of more benefit to the community, if it were properly understood, than Chemistry—the Chemistry of Common Life.

There is a space yet unoccupied for an elementary work which shall give to non-scientific readers some practical information as to the chemical composition of articles of daily use, and as to their action in the various operations in which they are employed.

The public are the more ready for the application of this knowledge since Chemistry is taught in nearly all High Schools, and most persons have a dim idea of what some part of it means. To gather up these indistinct notions into a definite and practical form is the aim of this little book.

PREFACE.

There is, lingering in the air, a great awe of chemistry and chemical terms, an inheritance from the age of alchemy. Every chemist can recall instances by the score in which manufacturers have asked for recipes for making some substitute for a well-known article, and have expected the most absurd results to follow the simple mixing of two substances. Chemicals are supposed by the multitude to be all-powerful, and great advantage is taken of this credulity by unscrupulous manufacturers.

The number of patent compounds thrown upon the market under fanciful and taking names is a witness to the apathy of housekeepers. It is time that they should bestir themselves for their own protection. A little knowledge of the right kind cannot hurt them, and it will surely bring a large return in comfort and economy.

These mysterious chemicals are not so many or so complicated in structure but that a little patient study will enable any one to understand the laws of their action, so far as they apply to the common operations of the household.

No attempt is here made to cover the whole ground of chemical science, but only to explain such of its principles as are involved in the raising of bread, and in a few other common processes.

PREFACE

To the Second Edition.

THE science of chemistry has made rapid strides in the past fifteen years. Biological science has sprung from infancy to sturdy manhood during the same time, and a knowledge of both with their relations to each other is necessary to the right understanding of the manifold operations of life. All the sciences and all the arts are taxed by the intelligent home-maker for the proper foundation and continuance of the complex life of the home.

The establishment of more homes and their right conduct when established, which results in the better utilization of time, money and strength, means the perpetuity, prosperity and power of the nation.

Without trespassing upon the domain of household bacteriology, a knowledge of the chemistry of cooking and cleaning must include some discussion of the sources of dirt, its composition and its dangers, and the discussion of methods for its removal, which shall at the same time be speedy, safe and effectual.

Experience teaches that in domestic work there is no *best* rule of universal application. Circumstances vary so widely that principles, alone, can be laid down. Each case requires a large proportion of judgment—a compound of more complex composition than any chemical substance ever dealt with.

If any housekeeper finds a method better for her purpose than the one specified here, let her keep to its use and tell it to others. This work will have accomplished its purpose if it interests those who understand already the principles of cooking and cleaning; gives a few answers to those who continually ask "Why?" and "How?" and stimulates to study and thought the many who have long labored with willing hearts but with untrained minds and hands.

Boston, 1897.

CONTENTS.

	PAGE
PREFACE TO FIRST EDITION	iii
PREFACE TO SECOND EDITION	v

PART I.

I.	MATTER AND ITS COMPOSITION	1
II.	ELEMENTARY CHEMISTRY	9
III.	STARCHES, SUGARS, FATS, THEIR PREPARATION AS FOOD	24
IV.	NITROGENOUS CONSTITUENTS	47
V.	FLAVORS AND CONDIMENTS. DIET	56

PART II.

I.	DUST	71
II.	DUST MIXTURES (GREASE AND DUST)	87
III.	STAINS, SPOTS, TARNISH	100
IV.	LAUNDRY	118
V.	CHEMICALS FOR HOUSEHOLD USE	145

BOOKS OF REFERENCE	153
INDEX	155

THE CHEMISTRY OF COOKING AND CLEANING.

CHAPTER I.

MATTER AND ITS COMPOSITION.

WE give the name matter to the objects which can be recognized by any one of our senses. There are many kinds of matter and many forms of one kind. Ice melts into water, water changes into steam. In our stoves, the hard, black coal disappears, leaving a soft, gray ash, that weighs much less than the original coal. Something has been taken away. *Matter.*

The leaf is covered by wind-blown soil and soon no leaf is there; but the matter of which it was composed is still somewhere, for that is never lost. Living matter is in constant change from one form to another. Our bodies are composed of matter, and to their continued existence, as well as to their growth, material substances are necessary. Some changes come quickly, some slowly. Years, ages even, are sometimes necessary to bring a result that is visible to us. *Changes in Matter.*

A familiar substance, sugar, for example, may be subjected to different changes. Put two tablespoonfuls of white sugar into a scant half cup of water. The sugar disappears. The clear water changes to a syrupy liquid. If the water is allowed to evaporate slowly, the sugar is found to remain.

A teaspoonful of sugar dropped upon the warm stove changes in character. There appears a black mass, which is readily recognized as charcoal.

Add a solution of an acid to a solution of an alkali, and observe that the acid substance and the alkaline substance are no longer in existence as such. There is, instead, a neutral saline substance dissolved in water. The new substance has the properties of neither of the others. The acid and the alkali have lost their identity.

Dissolve a teaspoonful of sugar in a cupful of water. Add a very little yeast and put the cup in a warm place. Soon bubbles of gas rise and break on the surface; while, on distilling the liquid, a new acquaintance presents itself in the form of alcohol. The first-mentioned change in the sugar is a physical change—the character of the substance is not permanently altered. The second is a chemical change—the substance loses its individual character. The third change in the sugar, most important for our present purpose, combines chemical and physical changes caused by the action of life. When the syrup "sours" or ferments, we know that living organisms are at work in the solution, changing the substance by their own processes of growth. To this class, then, we may apply the name biological change. Here belong the changes in our own bodies which enable them to live and grow. Death comes when these "vital" changes can no longer proceed in a normal, healthy manner.

Changes in matter, then, are of two kinds.

I. Physical. Change of form, without change of character. This is brought about by outside forces: heat, blows, etc.

II. Chemical. Change of character, with or without change of form. This is brought about by chemical agencies, by fire and electricity—also forces from without.

Physical and chemical forces, working together, allow of biological results, caused by living cells producing energy or force by means of their life processes.

Under these heads come the numerous changes which every housewife observes and which all should understand, so far as such understanding is necessary for the true economy of the house.

We have seen that matter is subject to two kinds of change. Experience teaches that matter exists in three different forms—solids, liquids and gases. <small>Forms of Matter.</small>

It teaches, also, that by the action of outside forces some solids become liquids and some liquids become gases. The reverse process, also, is known —gases change into liquids and liquids into solids. The chemist or physicist is able to change matter from one form into another in many more instances than are observed in ordinary experience.

Forces Causing Change in Latter.

What force, or forces, cause or can be made to cause these changes? Before an iron kettle or stove can be made, the metal from which it is formed must be subjected to intense heat, when it will become a liquid and can be poured into molds of any desired shape. The solid ice melts or becomes water at a low temperature; but at a higher degree of temperature, the water becomes steam or gas. Some solids, as camphor and iodine sublime, that is, pass directly into the gaseous form.

Heat, then, is one force which brings about a change of state in material substances. If heat be abstracted from a liquid, the latter may become a solid, as when water becomes ice. Like changes are less readily brought about by pressure, gases becoming liquids; liquids becoming solids. Cold and pressure, acting together, are able to liquefy the air even, and other gases once called permanent.

The forces exerted from without, then, are pressure, and the addition or subtraction of heat.

COOKING AND CLEANING. 5

Experience teaches that solid and liquid matter may be divided into smaller and smaller divisions until the particles are no longer visible under a powerful microscope. The scientist is led by his observations to the belief that matter is made up of infinitesimal particles or *atoms* and that chemical changes take place among these atoms and groups of atoms. They are invisible and indestructible. Each atom occupies space and has weight. Two or more atoms united make a *molecule*, which also is very far from being visible. It may be composed of two or more atoms of the same substance or many atoms of different substances. Atoms and Molecules.

In the social world there are individuals, families and communities; so in the material world there are atoms, simple molecules and complex groups of molecules. The groups or molecules are always separated from each other by greater or less distances. If the groups are many and the distances between them infinitely small, there is a "solid crowd." There must be some force to widen the distance between the groups and make them free to move among themselves. A layer of fat is a crowded mass of molecules—a solid. Heat drives the molecules apart, increases the distance between them, gives them a chance to move more freely and produces, thus, the liquid condi- States of Matter.

tion. Still further separation, with the breaking up of certain groups causes a freedom of movement in any and all directions, giving a gas or gases. If not restrained, these may pass entirely beyond our ken though still existent, for "matter cannot be created or destroyed at will."

Different degrees of heat produce varying degrees of liquefaction. The molecules may be given only a slight freedom of movement, causing a semi-liquid state, as in the melting of solder, of gelatine, and of tar. When the molecules are driven further apart the mass necessarily occupies more space. This is expansion. All matter expands or occupies more space under the action of heat; but in gases, the proportion of expansion is much the greatest, for the molecules have perfect freedom of movement. This expansion of gases with heat makes possible the process of ventilation by means of an open fire, and is one factor in the rise of dough.

Into these molecular spaces, molecules of other substances may enter. The molecules of solids, however, do not readily pass between one another in this way. The solids must be changed to liquids, that their molecules may have freedom of movement. This is commonly brought about by solution.

The degree of solubility of any substance de-

COOKING AND CLEANING.

pends largely upon the temperature of the solvent. Common salt dissolves nearly as well in cold as in warm water. "Soda" and alum dissolve more readily in warm than in cold, while cream of tartar requires hot water for its complete solution.

The amount of solid which water will dissolve usually increases with the temperature to a certain degree. After this no more will dissolve and the solution is "saturated." Gases readily dissolve in water, but, usually, in cold solutions only. *Saturation.*

The action of the liquid is increased if the solid be first powdered, for a greater area is thus presented to the action of the liquid. It is usually more rapid when the powder is placed upon the surface. Under these conditions each particle, while dissolving is surrounded by a thin envelop of syrup, which becomes heavier and sweeter. The film of syrup is washed away by the solvent liquid, so that a clean surface is continually exposed to be acted upon. Some particles are so light that they will not sink; then the process of solution is very slow. Solution is a valuable agent in bringing about chemical action during many processes of cooking and cleaning.

Water is a nearly universal solvent. It dissolves larger quantities of more substances than any other liquid. Some solids, however, dissolve *Solvents.*

more readily in other liquids, as camphor in alcohol. Silver, copper and tin are not perceptibly dissolved in pure water, while most of their compounds, as nitrate of silver and sulphate of copper, are thus soluble. Lead dissolves more readily in pure water than in that containing some impurities. Gold may be dissolved in a warm mixture of two strong acids. Many of these metallic solutions which may be formed in cooking utensils and water pipes are poisonous, and a knowledge of them becomes a matter of great importance to all housekeepers.

Swelling."
A process of daily occurrence in the household greatly resembles solution. It consists in the taking up of water, which produces an increase of bulk or "swelling," but no true solution. Gelatine swells in cold water and may then be dissolved in hot water. Starch "jells" by taking up water; so we soak the cereals which consist largely of starch, that they may be more quickly acted upon by heat.

CHAPTER II.

Elementary Chemistry.

MOST substances with which we deal in ordinary life are compounds of two or more elementary constituents. The grain of wheat, the flesh of animals, the dangerous poison, are each capable of separation into simpler substances. Finally a substance is found which cannot be divided without losing its identity. The chemical *element* is that substance out of which nothing essentially different has ever yet been obtained.

Pure gold is an element from which nothing can be taken different from itself, but gold coin contains a little copper or silver or both. The oxygen of the air is an element. Air is a mixture of two or more elements. Oxygen and hydrogen, both gaseous elements, unite in certain proportions to form the chemical compound, water. *[margin: Elements.]*

There are about eighty of these elements known to the chemist, while their compounds are infinite. For his convenience the chemist abbreviates the names of the elements into symbols which he uses instead of the names. Usually, the first or the first two letters of the Latin name are taken.

These symbols mean much more, however, than time saved, as we shall see.

Most of the elements unite with each other. Then in the resulting compounds, one or more elements may be exchanged for others, so that a multitude of combinations are formed out of few elementary substances. The bulk of our food, clothing and furniture is made up of only five or six of these elements, although about twenty of them enter into the compounds used in the household. The others are found in nature, in the chemical laboratory or in the physician's medicine case. A few are so rare as to be considered curiosities.

Every housewife should understand something of these chemical substances—their common forms, their nature and their reactions, that she may not be cheated out of time and money, and, more important still, that she may preserve the health of those for whom she cares.

All chemical changes are governed by *laws*. Under like conditions, like results follow. No chemical sleight of hand can make one pound of washing soda do the work of two pounds, or one pound of flour make a third more bread at one time than at another.

It has been assumed that all compounds are formed by the union of atoms—those smallest homogeneous particles of matter. Each atom has

COOKING AND CLEANING. 11

its definite weight, which remains constant. This weight is known in chemistry as "atomic weight." No single atom can be weighed by itself, but it is found that hydrogen is the lightest substance known, so the weight of its atom is called *one*. All other substances are compared with this unit, i. e., their atoms weigh one, two, three or more times the hydrogen atom.

Reckoned in this way the atom of oxygen weighs sixteen and the carbon atom twelve times as much as the atom of hydrogen. The symbol of an element, then, represents its constant atomic weight; so that, while the word *oxygen* means only the collection of properties to which is given the name, the symbol O indicates a definite quantity which is sixteen times the weight of the H atom. Chemical Symbols.

The *number* of atoms used is indicated by a small figure placed below and at the right of the symbol. When no figure appears, one atom is understood. In a compound, the number of *molecules* is designated by a large figure at the left of the formula: H_2SO_4 means one *molecule* containing two *atoms* of hydrogen, one of sulphur, four of oxygen. $4H_2SO_4$ means four *molecules* containing eight *atoms* of hydrogen, four of sulphur, sixteen of oxygen. A little chemical arithmetic is needed to compute the weight of these molecules. Molecular weight is the sum of the atomic weights of the constituent elements. Our chemical example then stands:

$$\begin{array}{r} \text{Two atoms of } H = 2 \\ \text{One atom of } S = 32 \\ \text{Four atoms of } O = 64 \\ \hline \text{One molecule of } H_2SO_4 = 98 \\ \text{Four molecules of } H_2SO_4 = 392 \end{array}$$

392 what? All weights are referred to the standard H; so the four molecules weigh 392 times as much as the hydrogen atom.

The symbols, then, are the chemist's shorthand alphabet, or his sign language. The non-scientific reader is apt to look upon the acquisition of this sign language as the schoolboy regards the study of Chinese—as the work of a lifetime. He would be near the truth were he to attempt to remember the symbols of all the complicated compounds known and constantly increasing; but a study of the properties and combinations of the few which make the common substances of daily use need not frighten the most busy housewife, for they can be comprehended in a few hours of thoughtful reading. Then a little practice will make them as familiar as the recipe of her favorite cake. "To master the symbolical language of chemistry, so as to fully understand what it ex-

COOKING AND CLEANING. 13

presses, is a great step toward mastering the science."

Having thus prepared the ground and collected materials, the foundation may be laid—i. e., the *laws* of chemical combination. It has been said that the elements unite with each other and exchange places one with another. In society there are persons whose powers of attraction toward others vary widely. In conversation upon any subject, one person may interest, with ease, one individual; another may hold two interested listeners; while a few, with rare gifts, may hold together a group of many. We say the last person has a stronger holding power than the other two. This may serve to illustrate what is known by experiment to be a fact among atoms. The chemist finds an atom of one element holding to itself one atom of a different element; another, holding two; while a third may hold three or more.

<small>Laws of Combination.</small>

Chlorine will hold to itself only one atom of H, making HCl, muriatic acid; but O holds two—H_2O—water; N holds three—NH_3—ammonia; and C, four—CH_4—"fire damp."

Under different conditions, some elements show different powers of attraction toward the same element; so again this chemical society resembles social life. Sometimes N will hold to itself one atom of O, sometimes two, and sometimes three with an atom of H besides.

Valence.

The chemist must understand all these holding powers, which he calls the *valence* of an element; but to him the housewife may leave the thorough knowledge, while she recognizes that by virtue of this *valence*, compounds are formed with widely different qualities; thus, H_2O is pure water, while H_2O_2, hydrogen peroxide, is a disinfectant and a bleaching agent; SO_2, sulphur dioxide, used for bleaching straw and fabrics, also a germicide, is a gas; while SO_3 is a white crystalline solid.

Unit of Value.

Valence is a variable quality, but in uniting, or exchanging places with each other, the atoms of each element have a value which remains constant. This value is expressed in terms of a certain unit which chemists have chosen as a standard.

At the outposts of the Hudson's Bay Territory all trade is on a system of barter or exchange, and therefore a basis of value is necessary. The skin of a beaver is agreed upon as the unit from which to count all values. A red fox skin is worth two beaver skins; a silver fox skin is worth four beaver skins. All the hunter's transactions are based upon these values. If he wishes to purchase a knife, he must pay four beaver skins; a gun will cost him three silver fox or twelve beaver skins.

Exchange Value.

The chemist's standard of value is the *atomic weight of hydrogen*. They choose this because it is the smallest relative weight known to enter into

COOKING AND CLEANING. 15

combination with other elements. Having once accepted this arbitrary choice, all values are counted from its value. For the convenience of the reader, this exchangeable value will be indicated by Roman numerals over the symbols in the formulæ given in this book, although this practice is not universal.

The exchange value of other elements is found by experiment. For our present purpose, these elements may be divided into three classes with hydrogen for a connecting link.

Combinations.

Exchange Values.

Table I.

Some common elements which unite with H:

$$
\left.\begin{array}{l}
\text{Chlorine} \dotfill Cl^I \\
\text{Iodine} \dotfill I^I \\
\text{Bromine} \dotfill Br^I \\
\text{Oxygen} \dotfill O^{II} \\
\text{Sulphur} \dotfill S^{II} \\
\text{Nitrogen} \dotfill N^{III} \\
\text{Carbon} \dotfill C^{IV}
\end{array}\right\} + H^I
$$

H^I unites with Cl^I, atom for atom, their values being the same. O^{II} unites with two of H^I, its value being twice that of H^I; while N^{III} equals three of H^I; and C^{IV}, four.

Table II.

Some common elements which unite with each other and with compounds of H.

Carbon ....C^{IV}
Oxygen ....O^{II}
Sodium ....Na^{I}
Potassium ....K^{I}
Calcium ....Ca^{II}
Chlorine ....Cl^{I}
Nitrogen ....N^{III}
Sulphur ....S^{II}
Phosphorus ....P^{V}

C^{IV} unites with O_2^{II} making $C^{IV}O_2^{II}$, carbon dioxide or carbonic acid gas; $C^{IV}O_2^{II}$ unites with $H_2^{I}O^{II}$ forming $H_2^{I}C^{IV}O_3^{II}$, carbonic acid gas in solution. Ca^{II} unites with O^{II}, forming $Ca^{II}O^{II}$, quicklime; $Ca^{II}O^{II}$ unites with $H_2^{I}O^{II}$, forming $Ca^{II}H_2^{I}O_2^{II}$, slaked lime.

Table III.

Some common elements which may be substituted for H in a compound, thereby making a new compound:

Sodium ....Na^{I}
Potassium ....K^{I}
Calcium ....Ca^{II}
Carbon ....C^{IV}

COOKING AND CLEANING.   17

Phosphorus ....P^{III} or P^{V}
Tin ....Sn^{II} or Sn^{IV}
Zinc ....Zn^{II}
Sulphur ....S^{II}
Copper ....Cu^{II}
Lead ....Pb^{II}
Gold ....Au^{III}
Aluminum ....Al^{II} or Al^{IV}

$H^{I}Cl^{I}$ is muriatic or hydrochloric acid. As Na^{I} has the same value as H^{I}, it may be substituted for it, and we have $Na^{I}Cl^{I}$, common salt. $H_2^{I}C^{IV}O_3^{II}$ is carbonic acid in solution. Na_2^{I} may be substituted for the H_2^{I} forming $Na_2^{I}C^{IV}O_3^{II}$, the commercial soda ash. Soda ash added to water and allowed to crystallize from it gives the familiar "washing crystals." $H^{I}N^{III}O_3^{II}$ is nitric acid. One atom of K^{I} will replace the H^{I}, forming $K^{I}N^{III}O_3^{II}$, or saltpetre.

Some of the compounds formed by the union and exchange of these various elements are very familiar substances. *Union and Exchange.*

"In the laboratory we never mix our materials at random, but always weigh out the exact proportions . . . for, if the least excess of one or the other substance over the proportions indicated is taken, that excess will be wasted. It will not enter into the chemical change."* It is this exact-

*"The New Chemistry," p. 151.

ness in dealing with matter which gives to the study of chemistry its great value from an educational standpoint. In the economy of nature nothing is lost. Wood and coal burn in our stoves. The invisible product of their combustion, $C^{IV}O_2^{II}$, passes into the air, but adds a definite amount to the weight of the air. Twelve pounds of coal (free from ash) in burning take from the air thirty-two pounds of oxygen and give back to the air forty-four pounds of carbon dioxide.

Water. Water is always composed of two atoms of hydrogen to one of oxygen, whether the quantity formed be one molecule or one million molecules. The water molecule, $H_2^I O^{II}$ (atomic weights, $H_2^I = 2$, $O^{II} = 16$) weighs 18, then for every eighteen parts by weight of water, there will be two parts by weight of H^I and sixteen parts by weight of O^{II}.

Chemical Equations. $C^{IV}O_2^{II}$, carbon dioxide, has one atom of carbon and two atoms of oxygen in each molecule; while by weight, twelve parts are C^{IV} and thirty-two are O^{II}. The exchanges and interchanges among the elements according to these two laws of *value* and *weight* form chemical reactions. The written expression of the reaction is called a chemical equation. In all chemical equations there is just as much weight represented on one side of the sign of equality ($=$) as on the other.

COOKING AND CLEANING. 19

$$C^{IV} + O_2^{II} = C^{IV}O_2^{II}$$
$$12 + 32 = 44$$
Carbon. Oxygen. Carbon Dioxide.

$H^I Cl^I$ + $Na^I O^{II} H^I$ = $Na^I Cl^I$ + $H_2^I O^{II}$
Muriatic Acid.   Caustic Soda.   Sodium, Chloride or Common Salt.   Water.

$$36.5 + 40 = 58.5 + 18$$
$$76.5 = 76.5$$

This shows that the sum of the weights of the two substances taken is equal to the sum of the weights of the new substances formed as the result of the reaction. These facts lead up to one of the fundamental laws of the present science of chemistry—the Law of Definite Proportions: *In any chemical compound the elements always unite in the same definite proportion by weight.* Law of Definite Proportions.

The atomic weights of elements united in a compound are then spoken of as the combining weights; thus, twelve and thirty-two are the combining weights of C^{IV} and O^{II}. Out of this first law grows a second—the Law of Multiple Proportions: *When elements form more than one compound, they unite according to some multiple of their combining weights.* Law of Multiple Proportions.

As we have noticed, sulphur and oxygen form different compounds—SO_2 and SO_3—where the combining weights are thirty-two to thirty-two

20   THE CHEMISTRY OF

for the first and thirty-two to forty-eight for the second.

These two laws are the corner-stones upon which all reactions are built. If we wish to obtain forty-four pounds of carbon dioxide (carbonic acid gas) we may, according to our first law, write out the reaction which we know will take place.

$$C + O_2 = CO_2$$

The combining weight of carbon is 12.
One atom = ...12
The combining weight of oxygen is 16.
Two atoms = ...32
                                    ——
$CO_2 =$ 44

Then we must take twelve pounds of carbon and thirty-two pounds of oxygen to make our desired forty-four pounds of gas.

Exchange of Groups. When more than two elements enter into combination, it is common for two or more to band together. In such a case the group has an exchange value of its own, which is not the sum of the values of its separate elements, but which is a constant value, dependent upon their values in a way which it is not necessary to explain here. These partnerships will be included in brackets, as $(SO_4)^{II}$, $(CO_3)^{II}$, $(NO_3)^{I}$. These groups do not represent actual compounds, which exist alone, like $H_2^{I}O^{II}$, $H^{I}Cl^{I}$, $C^{IV}O_2^{II}$, $Na^{I}Cl^{I}$; but the group enclosed by the brackets passes from one compound into another as if it were one element. The numeral over the bracketed letters indicates the exchange value of the partnership, not the sum of the elements. A few illustrations will make this clearer.

Table IV.

Mineral acids and some of their common compounds:

$H^I Cl^I$	$H^I(NO_3)^I$	$H_2^I(SO_4)^{II}$	$H_2(CO_3)^{II}$
Muriatic Acid.	Nitric Acid.	Sulphuric Acid.	Carbonic Acid.

Compounds:

$Na^I Cl^I$	$K^I(NO_3)^I$	$Ca^{II}(SO_4)^{II}$	$Ca^{II}(CO_3)^{II}$
Salt.	Saltpetre.	Plaster of Paris.	Marble.

Reactions among the above substances:

$$H_2^I(SO_4)^{II} + Ca^{II}(CO_3)^{II} = Ca^{II}(SO_4)^{II} + H_2^I(CO_3)^{II}$$

$$H_2^I(SO_4)^{II} + 2(Na^I Cl^I) = Na_2^I(SO_4)^{II} + 2(H^I Cl^I)^I$$

$$H_2^I(SO_4)^{II} + Na^I Cl^I = Na^I H^I(SO_4)^{II} + H^I Cl^I$$

It will be seen that the groups do not separate, but combine and exchange with the single elements by the same laws which govern the combinations among simpler substances.

The last two equations show how, where there are two atoms of hydrogen which may be replaced, either one or both can be exchanged for an atom of equal replacing value. The two compounds thus formed will differ in their properties. This will be more fully shown later on in the case of cream of tartar.

BAKING POWDERS.

$$\overset{I\ I\ II}{NaH(CO_3)} + \overset{I\ I}{HCl} = \overset{I\ I}{NaCl} + \overset{I\ II}{H_2(CO_3)} (\text{or } \overset{I\ II}{H_2O} + CO_2)$$
84   36.5   58.5   (44)
Soda.   Muriatic   Salt.   Water.   Carbonic
        Acid.   Acid Gas.

$$2\overset{I\ I\ II}{NaH(CO_3)} + \overset{I\ II}{H_2(C_4H_4O_6)} = \overset{I}{Na_2}(C_4H_4O_6) + \overset{I\ II}{H_2O} + 2CO_2$$
2 × 84   150   (2 × 44)
Soda.   Tartaric Acid.   Carbonic
                                             Acid Gas.

$$\overset{I\ I\ II}{NaH(CO_3)} + \overset{I\ II}{KH(C_4H_4O_6)} = \overset{I\ I}{KNa}(C_4H_4O_6) + \overset{I\ II}{H_2O} + CO_2$$
84   188   44
Soda.   Cream of Tartar.   Rochelle Salt.   Carbonic
                                                       Acid Gas.

$$6(\overset{I\ I\ II}{NaH(CO_3)}) + \overset{I\ II}{K_2Al_{2\,4}(SO_4)} = K_2SO_4 + 3(Na_2SO_4) + Al_2O_3 + 3H_2O + 6CO_2$$
6 × 84   517   6 × 44
Soda.   Alum.   Carbonic
                                                                            Acid Gas.

$$4(\overset{I\ I\ II}{NaH(CO_3)}) + 2(\overset{I\ II}{CaH_2(PO_4)}) = Na_4H_2(PO_4) + Ca_2H_2 2(PO_4) + 4CO_2 + 4H_2O$$
4 × 84   468   4 × 44
Soda.   Acid   Carbonic
      Phosphate.   Acid Gas.

CHAPTER III.

STARCHES, SUGARS, FATS, THEIR PREPARATION FOR FOOD.

Living and Lifeless Matter.

THE material world is divided into living and lifeless matter. All living matter requires food that it may grow, repair waste, and reproduce itself, if the existence of its kind is to be continued. This food must be made from the material elements we have been studying. Food for the human body must, therefore, contain such elements, in combination, as are found in the body substance, in order that new materials may be formed from them by the processes of life.

Chemical Change Produces Heat.

Wherever there is life, there is chemical change, and, as a rule, a certain degree of heat is necessary, in order that chemical change may occur. Vegetation does not begin in the colder climates until the air becomes warmed by the heat of the spring. When the cold of winter comes upon the land, vegetation ceases. If plant life is to be sustained during a northern winter, artificial warmth must be supplied. This is done by heat from a furnace or stove. In chemical terms, carbon and hydrogen from coal, wood, or gas are caused to unite with the oxygen of the air to form carbon dioxide (carbonic acid gas) and water, and

by this union of two elements with oxygen, heat is produced.
$$C^{IV}+O_2{}^{II}=C^{IV}O_2{}^{II}$$
$$C^{IV}H_4{}^{I}+O_4{}^{II}=C^{IV}O_2{}^{II}+2H_2{}^{I}O^{II}$$

These two chemical reactions indicate the changes which cause the production of artificial heat generally used for domestic purposes. All living matter, whether plant or animal, is found by analysis to contain carbon, oxygen, hydrogen, and nitrogen. Other elements are present in small and varying quantities, but "the great four" are the essentials. The plant is able to take all its food elements from air, water and soil, and, in its own cells, to manufacture those compounds upon which it can feed; while an animal cannot do this, but must accept for the most part the manufactured product of the plant. Man, therefore, finds his food in both vegetable and animal substances.

Combustion.

Since many animals live in temperatures in which plants would die, it is evident that they must have some source of heat in themselves. This is found in the union of the oxygen of the air breathed, with carbonaceous matter eaten as food, and the formation of carbonic acid gas (carbon dioxide), and water (CO_2 and H_2O), just as in the case of the combustion of the wood in the grate. Only, instead of this union taking place in one spot, and so rapidly as to be accompanied by light, as in the case of the grate fire, it takes place slowly and continuously in each living cell. Nevertheless, the chemical reaction seems to be identical.

Vital Temperature. The heat of the human body must be maintained at 37° C—the temperature necessary for the best performance of the normal functions. Any continued variation from this degree of heat indicates disease. Especially important is it that there be no considerable *lowering* of this temperature, for a fall of one degree is dangerous.

Food Elements for Combustion. The first requirement of animal life is, then, the food which supplies the heat necessary for the other chemical changes to take place. The class of foods which will be considered here as those utilized for the production of animal heat among other functions, includes the carbon compounds, chiefly composed of carbon, hydrogen and oxygen.

Oxygen. The slow combustion or oxidation of these carbonaceous bodies cannot take place without an abundance of oxygen; hence, the diet of the animal must include fresh air—a point too often overlooked. The amount of oxygen, by weight, taken in daily, is equal to the sum of all the other food elements. One-half of these consists of some form of starch or sugar—the so-called carbohydrates,

COOKING AND CLEANING. 27

in which the hydrogen and oxygen are found in the same proportions as in water. (The fats will be considered by themselves.)

Starches, sugars and gums are among the constituents of plants, and are sometimes found in animals in small quantities. Starch is found in greater or less abundance in all plants and is laid up in large quantities in the seeds of many species. Rice is nearly pure starch, wheat and the other cereals contain sixty to seventy per cent of it. Some tubers contain it, as potatoes, although in less quantity, ten to twenty per cent. It is formed by means of the living plant-cell and the sun's rays, from the carbon dioxide and water contained in the air, and it is the end of the plant life—the stored energy of the summer, prepared for the early life of the young plant another year. An allied substance is called cellulose. This occurs under numerous forms, in the shells and skins of fruits, in their membraneous partitions, and in the cell walls. Starch in its common forms is insoluble in water. It dissolves partially in boiling water, forming a transparent jelly when cooled.

Starches.

Sugars, also, are a direct or indirect product of plant life. Common sugar, or cane-sugar, occurs in the juices of a few grasses, as the sugar-cane; of some trees; and of some roots. Milk-sugar is

Sugars.

found in the milk of *mammalia*, while grape-sugar is a product of the ripening processes in fruit.

Digestion is primarily synonymous with solution. All solid food materials must become practically soluble before they can pass through the walls of the digestive system. As a rule, non-crystalline bodies are not diffusible, so that starch and like materials must be transformed into soluble, crystalline substances, before absorption can take place. Cane-sugar, too, has to undergo a chemical change before it can be absorbed; but grape and milk sugars are taken directly into the circulation. To this fact is due a part of the great nutritive value of dried fruits as raisins, dates and figs, and the value of milk-sugar over cane-sugar, for children or invalids. Chemically pure milk-sugar can now be obtained at wholesale for about 35 cents per pound. This may be used in certain diseases when cane-sugar is harmful. The chemical transformations of starch and sugar have been very carefully and scientifically studied with reference to brewing and wine-making. Several of the operations concerned necessitate great precision in respect to temperature and length of time, and these operations bear a close analogy to the process of bread-making by means of yeast. The general principles on which the conversion of starch into sugar, and sugar into alcohol, are con-

COOKING AND CLEANING. 29

ducted will therefore be stated as preliminary to a discussion of starch and sugar as food.

Starch Conversion. There are two distinct means known to the chemist, by which this change can be produced. One is by the use of acid and heat, which changes the starch into sugar, but can go no farther. The other is by the use of a class of substances called ferments, some of which have the power of changing the starch into sugar, and others of changing the sugar into alcohol and carbon dioxide. These ferments are in great variety and the seeds of some of them are always present in the air. Among the chemical substances called ferments, one is formed in sprouting grain which is called diastase or starch converter, which first, under the influence of warmth, changes the starch into a sugar, as is seen in the preparation of malt for brewing. The starch ($C_6H_{10}O_5$), first takes up water (H_2O), and, under the influence of the ferment, is changed into maltose. Cane-sugar is readily converted into two sugars, dextrose and levulose, belonging to the glucoses.

$$C_{12}^{IV}H_{22}^{I}O_{11}^{II} + H_2^{I}O^{II} + \text{ferment} = 2C_6^{IV}H_{12}^{I}O_6^{II}$$
Cane-Sugar.   Water.   Dextrose and Levulose.

Sugar Conversion. Glucose and maltose are converted by yeast into alcohol and carbon dioxide. In beer, the alcohol is the product desired, but in bread-making the chief object of the fermentation is to produce carbon dioxide to puff up the bread, while the alcohol escapes in the baking.

$$C_6^{IV}H_{12}^{I}O_6^{II} = \begin{cases} 2C_2^{IV}H_6^{I}O^{II} \text{ Alcohol.} \\ 2C^{IV}O_2^{II} \text{ Carbon Dioxide.} \end{cases}$$

The alcohol, if burned, would give carbon dioxide and water.

$$\underset{\text{Alcohol.}}{2C_2^{IV}H_6^{I}O^{II}} + \underset{\text{Oxygen.}}{12O^{II}} = \underset{\text{Carbon Dioxide.}}{4C^{IV}O_2^{II}} + \underset{\text{Water.}}{6H_2^{I}O^{II}}$$

It will be seen, from the previous equations, that nothing has been lost during the process. The six atoms of carbon in the original starch reappear in the carbon dioxide at the end, $2CO_2 + 4CO_2$. Two atoms of hydrogen from the water, and thirteen atoms of oxygen from the water and the air have been added. Reckoning the atomic weights of the starch used, the carbon dioxide and the water formed, we find that, in round numbers, sixteen pounds of starch will yield twenty-six pounds of gas and ten pounds of water, or more than double the weight of the starch. These products of decomposition are given back to the air in the same form in which those substances existed from which the starch was originally formed.

The same cycle of chemical changes goes on in the human body when starchy substances are

COOKING AND CLEANING. 31

taken as food. Such food, moistened and warmed in the mouth, becomes mixed with air through mastication, by reason of the property of the saliva to form froth, and also becomes impregnated with ptyalin, a substance which can change starch into sugar as can the diastase of the malt. The mass then passes into the stomach, and the change, once begun, goes on. As soon as the sugar is formed, it is absorbed into the circulatory system and, by the life processes, is oxidized, i. e., united with more oxygen and changed finally into carbon dioxide and water.

No starch is utilized in the human system as starch. It must undergo transformation before it can be absorbed. Therefore starchy foods must not be given to children before the secretion of the starch converting ferments has begun, nor to any one in any disease where the normal action of the glands secreting these ferments is interrupted. Whatever starch passes out of the stomach unchanged, meets a very active converter in the intestinal juice. If grains of starch escape these two agents, they leave the system in the same form as that in which they entered it.

Early man, probably, lived much like the beasts, taking his food in a raw state. Civilized man requires much of the raw material to be changed, by the action of heat, into substances more palatable and already partly digested.

The chemistry of cooking the raw materials is very simple. It is in the mixing of incongruous materials in one dish or one meal that complication arises.

The Cooking of Starch.

Since fully one-half of our food is made up of starches and sugars, it is pertinent to examine, beside their chemical composition, the changes which they may undergo in the processes of cooking that can render them more valuable as food, or which, on the other hand, may in large measure destroy their food value.

The cooking of starch, as rice, farina, etc., requires little explanation. The starch grains are prepared by the plant to keep during a season of cold or drought and are very close and compact; they need to be swollen and distended by moisture in order that the chemical change may take place readily, as it is a law, that the finer the particles, the sooner a given change takes place, as has been explained in a previous chapter. Starch grains may increase to twenty-five times their bulk during the process of hydration.

The cooking of the potato and other starch-containing vegetables, is likewise a mechanical process very necessary as a preparation for the chemical action of digestion; for raw starch has been shown to require a far longer time and more digestive power than cooked starch. Change takes place slowly, even with thorough mastication, unless the starch is heated and swollen, and, in case the intestinal secretion is disturbed, the starch may not become converted at all.

The most important of all the articles of diet which can be classed under the head of starchy foods is bread. Wheat bread is not all starch, but it contains a larger percentage of starch than of anything else, and it must be discussed under this topic. Bread of some kind has been used by mankind from the first dawn of civilization. During the earlier stages, it consisted chiefly of powdered meal and water, baked in the sun, or on hot stones. This kind of bread had the same characteristics as the modern sea-biscuit, crackers and hoe-cake, as far as digestibility was concerned. It had great density, it was difficult to masticate, and the starch in it presented but little more surface to the digestive fluids than that in the hard compact grain, the seed of the plant. *[margin: Bread.]*

Experience must have taught the semi-civilized man that a light porous loaf was more digestible than a dense one. Probably some dough was accidentally left over, yeast plants settled upon it from the air, fermentation set in, and the possibility of porous bread was thus suggested.

The small loaf, light, spongy, with a crispness and sweet, pleasant taste, is not only æsthetically, but chemically, considered the best form in which starch can be presented to the digestive organs. The porous condition is desired in order that as large a surface as possible shall be presented to the action of the chemical converter, the ptyalin of the saliva, and, later, to other digestive ferments. There is also a better aëration in the process of mastication.

Ideal Bread.

The ideal bread for daily use should fulfill certain dietetic conditions:

1. It should retain as much as possible of the nutritive principles of the grain from which it is made.

2. It should be prepared in such a manner as to secure the complete assimilation of these nutritive principles.

3. It should be light and porous, so as to allow the digestive juices to penetrate it quickly and thoroughly.

4. It should be especially palatable, so that one may be induced to eat enough for nourishment.

5. It should be nearly or quite free from coarse bran, which causes too rapid muscular action to allow of complete digestion. This effect is also produced when the bread is sour.

Ordinary Graham bread, brown bread and the black bread of Germany fulfill conditions 1 and 4, but fail in the other three. Bakers' bread of fine

COOKING AND CLEANING.

white flour fulfills 2, 3 and 5, but fails in the other two. Home-made bread often fulfills conditions 4 and 5, but fails in the other three.

Very early in the history of the human race leavened bread seems to have been used. This was made by allowing flour and water to stand in a warm place until fermentation had well set in. A portion of this dough was used to start the process anew in fresh portions of flour and water. This kind of bread had to be made with great care, for germs different from yeast might get in, forming lactic acid—the acid of sour milk—and other substances unpleasant to the taste and harmful to the digestion.

Leaven or Yeast.

Butyric acid occurs in rancid butter and in many putrified organic substances. A sponge made from perfectly pure yeast and kept pure may stand for a long time after it is ready for the oven and still show no sign of sourness.

On account of the disagreeable taste of leaven and because of the possibility that the dough might reach the stage of putrid fermentation, chemists and physicians sought for some other means of rendering the bread light and porous. The search began almost as soon as chemistry was worthy the name of a science, and one of the early patents bears the date 1837. Much time and thought have been devoted to the perfecting of unfermented bread; but since the process of beer-making has been universally introduced, yeast has been readily obtained, and is an effectual means of giving to the bread a porous character and a pleasant taste. Since the chemistry of the yeast fermentation has been better understood, a change of opinion has come about, and nearly all scientific and medical men now recommend fermented bread.

The bacteriology of bread and bread-making is yet somewhat obscure. The ordinary yeasts are so mingled with bacteria that the part which each plays is not yet understood. Only experiments long continued will solve these problems.

Chemical Reactions in Bread-Making. The chemical reactions concerned in bread-raising are similar to those in beer-making. To the flour and warmed water is added yeast, a microscopic plant, capable of causing the alcoholic fermentation. The yeast begins to act at once, but slowly; more rapidly if sugar has been added and the dough is a semi-fluid. Without the addition of sugar no change is evident to the eye for some hours, as the fermentation of sugar from starch, by the diastase, gives rise to no gaseous products. As soon as the sugar is decomposed by the yeast plant into alcohol and carbonic acid gas (carbon dioxide), the latter product makes itself known by the bubbles which appear and the consequent swelling of the whole mass.

It is the carbon dioxide which causes the sponge-like condition of the loaf by reason of the peculiar tenacity of the gluten, one of the constituents of wheat. It is a well-known fact that no other kind of grain will make so light a bread as wheat. It is the right proportion of gluten (a nitrogenous substance to be considered later) which enables the light loaf to be made of wheat flour.

The production of carbon dioxide is the end of the *chemical* process. The rest is purely mechanical. The kneading is for the purpose of rendering the dough elastic by the spreading out of the already fermented mass and its thorough incorporation with the fresh flour. Another reason for kneading is, that the bubbles of gas may be broken up into as small portions as possible, in order that there may be no large holes, only very fine ones, evenly distributed through the loaf, when it is baked.

The temperature at which the dough should be maintained during the chemical process is an important point. If the characteristics of "home-made" bread are desired, it is found to be better to use a small amount of yeast and to keep the dough at a temperature from 55 degrees to 60 degrees for twelve to fifteen hours, than to use a larger quantity of yeast and to cause its rapid growth. The changes which produce the desired effect are not fully under-

Temperature of Bread-Making.

stood. Above 90 degrees the production of acetic acid—the acid of vinegar—is liable to occur: for this temperature, while unfavorable for the yeast plant, is favorable for the growth of the particular bacterium which produces acetic acid.

$$C_2^{IV}H_6^{I}O^{II} + O_2^{II} = C_2^{IV}H_4^{I}O_2^{II} + H_2^{I}O^{II}$$
Alcohol.   Acetic   Water.
Acid.

After the dough is stiffened by a little fresh flour and is nearly ready for the oven, the temperature may be raised, for a few minutes, to 100 degrees or 165 degrees F. The rapid change in the yeast is soon stopped by the heat of the oven.

Object of Baking. The baking of the loaf has for its object to kill the ferment, to heat the starch sufficiently to render it easily soluble, to expand the carbon dioxide and drive off the alcohol, to stiffen the gluten, and to form a crust which shall have a pleasant flavor. The oven must be hot enough to raise the temperature of the *inside* of the loaf to 212 degrees F., or the bacteria will not all be killed. A pound loaf, four inches by four by nine, may be baked three-quarters of an hour in an oven where the initial temperature is 400 degrees F., or for an hour and a half, where the temperature during the time does not rise above 350 degrees F. Quick baking gives a white loaf, because the starch has undergone but little change.

The long, slow baking gives a yellow tint, with the desirable nutty flavor, and crisp crust. Different flavors in bread are supposed to be caused by the different varieties of yeast used or by bacteria, which are present in all doughs, as ordinarily prepared.

The brown coloration of the crust, which gives a peculiar flavor to the loaf, is caused by the formation of substances analogous to dextrine and caramel, due to the high heat to which the starch is subjected.

One hundred pounds of flour are said to make from 126 to 150 pounds of bread. This increase of weight is due to the incorporation of water, possibly by a chemical union, as the water does not dry out of the loaf, as it does out of a sponge. The bread seems moist when first taken from the oven, and dry after standing some hours, but the weight will be found nearly the same. It is this probable chemical change which makes the difference, to delicate stomachs, between fresh bread and stale. A thick loaf is best when eaten after it is twenty-four hours old, although it is said to be "done" when ten hours have passed. Thin biscuits do not show the same ill effects when eaten hot. The bread must be well baked in any case, in order that the process of fermentation may be stopped. If this be stopped and the mastication be thorough, so that

40   THE CHEMISTRY OF

the bread is in finely divided portions instead of in a mass or ball, the digestibility of fresh and stale bread is about the same.

Expansion of Water into Steam.

The expansion of water or ice into seventeen hundred times its volume of steam is sometimes taken advantage of in making snow-bread, water-gems, etc. It plays a part in the lightening of pastry and crackers. Air, at 70 degrees, doubles its volume at a temperature of 560° F., so that if air is entangled in a mass of dough, it gives a certain lightness when the whole is baked. This is the cause of the sponginess of cakes made with eggs. The viscous albumen catches the air and holds it, even when it is expanded, unless the oven is too hot, when the sudden expansion is liable to burst the bubbles and the cake falls.

As has been said, the production of the porous condition, by means of carbon dioxide, generated in some other way than by the decomposition of starch, was the study of practical chemists for some years.

Methods of Obtaining Carbon dioxide.

A simple method for obtaining the carbon dioxide is by heating bicarbonate of sodium.

$$2Na^I H^I C^{IV} O_3^{II} + heat = Na_2^I C^{IV} O_3^{II} + H_2^I O^{II} + C^{IV} O_2^{II}$$

The bicarbonate splits up into sodium carbonate, water, and carbon dioxide. The bread is light but yellow. Some of the carbonate remains in the bread, and as it neutralizes the acid of the gastric juice, digestion may be retarded. It also acts upon the gluten producing an unpleasant odor.

Among the first methods proposed was one undoubtedly the best theoretically, but very difficult to put in practice, viz., the liberation of carbon dioxide from bicarbonate of sodium by means of muriatic acid.

$$Na^IH^IC^{IV}O_3^{II} + H^IC^{I} = Na^IC^{I} + H_2^IO^{II} + C^{IV}O_2^{II}$$

"Soda." Hydrochloric Common Salt. Water. Carbon dioxide.
Acid.

This liberation of gas is instantaneous on the contact of the acid with the "soda," and only a skilled hand can mix the bread and place it in the oven without the loss of much of the gas. Tartaric acid, the acid phosphates, sour milk (lactic acid), vinegar (acetic acid), alum—all of which have been used—are open to the same objection. Cream of tartar is the only acid substance commonly used which does not liberate the gas by simple contact when cold. It unites with "soda" only when heated, because it is so slightly soluble in cold water. For the even distribution of the gas by thorough mixing, cream of tartar would seem to be the best; but as, beside gas, there are other products which remain behind in the bread in the case of all the so-called baking powders, the healthfulness of these residues must be considered.

Common salt is the safest, and perhaps the residues from acid phosphate are next in order.

The tartrate, lactate and acetate of sodium are not known to be especially hurtful. As the important constituent of Seidlitz powders is Rochelle salt, the same compound as that resulting from the use of cream of tartar and "soda," it is not likely to be very deleterious, taken in the small quantities in which even habitual "soda biscuit" eaters take it.

Injurious Products. The various products formed by the chemical decomposition of alum and "soda" are possibly the most injurious, as the sulphates are supposed to be the least readily absorbed salts. Taking into consideration the advantage given by the insolubility of cream of tartar in cold water, and the comparatively little danger from its derivative—Rochelle salt—it would seem to be, on the whole, the best substance to add to the soda in order to liberate the gas; but the proportions should be chemically exact, in order that there be no excess of alkali to hinder digestion. Hence, baking powders prepared by weight and carefully mixed, are a great improvement over cream of tartar and "soda" measured separately. As commonly used, the proportion of soda should be a little less than half. The table on page 23 gives the chemical reactions of the more common baking powders.

FATS.

Another group of substances which, by their slow combustion or oxidation in the animal body, yield carbon dioxide and water and furnish heat to the system, is called fats. These comprise the animal fats—suet, lard, butter, etc.—and the vegetable oils—olive oil, cottonseed oil, the oily matter in corn, oats, etc.

Fats, ordinarily so called, are simply solidified oils, and oils are liquid fats. The difference between them is one of temperature only; for, within the body, all are fluid. In this fluid condition, they are held in little cells which make up the fatty tissues.

These fatty materials all have a similar composition, containing, when pure, only carbon, hydrogen, and oxygen. They differ from starch and sugar in the proportion of oxygen to the carbon and hydrogen, there being very little oxygen relatively in the fatty group, hence more must be taken from the air for their combustion.

Composition of Fats.

$$C_{18}{}^{IV}H_{36}{}^{I}O_2{}^{II} \qquad C_6{}^{IV}H_{10}{}^{I}O_5{}^{II}$$
Stearic Acid in Suet.   Starch.

One pound of starch requires one and two-tenths pounds of oxygen, while one pound of suet requires about three pounds of oxygen for perfect combustion. This combination of oxygen with the

Combustion of Fats.

excess of hydrogen, as well as with the excess of carbon results in a greater quantity of heat from fat, pound for pound, than can be obtained from starch or sugar. Recent experiments have proved that the fats yield more than twice as much heat as the carbohydrates; hence people in Arctic regions require large amounts of fat, and, everywhere, the diet of winter should contain more fat than that of summer.

Sources of Energy.

While the chemical expression of these changes is that of heat produced, it must be remembered that energy or work done by the body is included, and that both fats and carbohydrates are the source of this energy, and that they must be increased in proportion as the mechanical work of the body increases. If a quantity is taken at any one time greater than the body needs for its work, the surplus will be deposited as a bank account, to be drawn from in case of any lack in the future supply of either.

This double source of energy has a large economic value, for it has been noticed that in communities where fats are dear, the required amount of heat-giving and energy-producing food is made up by a larger proportion of the cheaper carbohydrates. This prevents too large a draft on the bank account. It has also been noticed that wage-earners do use a large proportion of fat, whenever it is within their means.

COOKING AND CLEANING.   45

Numerous investigations into the condition of the insane, as well as of the criminal classes, show the results of too little nutrition and the absence of sufficient fat. The diet of school children should be carefully regulated with the fat supply in view. Girls, especially, show, at times, a dislike to fat and an overfondness for sugar. They should have the proper proportion of fat furnished by butter, cream, or, if need be, in disguised form. The cook must remember that the butter absorbed from her cake tin or the olive oil on her salad is food, as well as the flour and eggs.

Necessity of Fat in the Diet.

The essential oils, although very important, as will be shown in the chapter on flavors, occur in such small quantities that they need not be considered here, except by way of caution. These oils are all volatile, and, therefore, will be dissipated by a high temperature.

The digestion of fats is mainly a process of emulsion. With the intestinal fluids, the bile, especially, the fats form an emulsion in which the globules are finely divided, and rendered capable of passing through the membranes into the circulatory system. The change, if any, is not one destructive of the properties of the fatty matters.

If we define cooking as the application of heat, then whatever we do to fats in the line of cooking them is liable to hinder rather than help their diges-

The Digestion of Fat.

tibility. The flavor which cooking gives to food materials containing fat is, in general, due not to any flavor of the fat but to substances produced in the surrounding tissues.

Effect of High Temperature on Fats.

Fats may be heated to a temperature far above that of boiling water without showing any change; but there comes a point, different for each fat, where reactions take place, the products of which irritate the mucous membranes and, therefore, interfere with digestion. It is the volatile products of such decomposition which cause the familiar action upon the eyes and throat during the process of frying, and, also, the tell-tale odors throughout the house. The indigestibility of fatty foods, or foods cooked in fat, is due to these harmful substances produced by the too high temperature. It must not be inferred from what has been said that the oxidation of starch and fat is the only source of heat in the animal body. A certain quantity is undoubtedly derived from the chemical changes of the other portions of food, but the chemistry of these changes is not yet fully understood.

CHAPTER IV.

Nitrogenous Constituents.

THE animal body is a living machine, capable of doing work—raising weights, pulling loads, and the like. The work of this kind which it does can be measured by the same standard as the work of any machine, i. e., by the mechanical unit of energy—the foot-ton. <small>Animal Body a Machine.</small>

The power to do mechanical work comes from the consumption of fuel,—the burning of wood, coal or gas; and this potential energy of fuel is often expressed in units of heat or *calories*, a calorie being nearly the amount of heat required to raise two quarts of water *one* degree Fahrenheit. The animal body also requires its fuel, namely food, in order to do other work—its thinking, its talking or even its worrying. <small>Calories.</small>

The animal body is more than a machine. It requires fuel to enable it not only *to work* but also to *live*, even without working. About one-third of the food eaten goes to maintain its life, for while the inanimate machine is sent periodically to the repair-shop, the living machine must do its own <small>Need of Body Fuel.</small>

repairing, day by day, and minute by minute. Hence it is that the estimations of the fuel and repair material needed to keep the living animal body in good working and thinking condition are, in the present state of our knowledge, somewhat empirical; but it is believed that, within certain wide limits, useful calculations can be made by any one willing to give a little time and thought to the subject. Our knowledge may be rapidly increased if such study is made in many localities and under varying circumstances.

The adult animal lives, repairs waste, and does work; while the young animal does all these and more—it grows. For growth and work something else is needed beside starch and fat. The muscles are the instruments of motion, and they must grow and be nourished, in order that they may have power. The nourishment is carried to them by the blood in which, as well as in muscular tissue, there is found an element which we have not heretofore considered, namely, nitrogen. It has been proved that the wear and tear of the muscles and brain causes the liberation of nitrogenous compounds, which pass out of the system as such, and this loss must be supplied by the use of some kind of food which contains nitrogen. Starch and fat do not contain this element; therefore they cannot furnish it to the blood.

COOKING AND CLEANING.

Nitrogenous food-stuffs comprise at least two large groups, the Albumins or Proteids and the Albuminoids.

Nitrogenous Food-Stuffs.

ALBUMINS.

The *Albumins* in some form are never absent from animal and vegetable organisms. They are more abundant in animal flesh and in the blood. The typical food of this class is the white of egg, which is nearly pure albumin. Other common articles of diet belonging to this group are the casein of milk, the musculin of animal flesh, the gluten of wheat, and the legumin of peas and beans.

Egg albumin is soluble in cold water, but coagulates at about 160 degrees F. At this point it is tender, jelly-like, and easily digested, while at a higher temperature it becomes tough, hard and soluble with difficulty.

The albumin of flesh is contained largely in the blood; therefore the juices of meat extracted in cold water form an albuminous solution. If this be heated to the right temperature the albumin is coagulated and forms the "scum" which many a cook skims off and throws away. In doing this she wastes a large portion of the nutriment. She should retain this nutrition in the meat by the quick coagulation of the albumin of the exterior, which will prevent further loss, or use the nutritive solution in the form of soups or stews. "Clear soups" have lost much of their nutritive value and, therefore, belong among the luxuries.

ALBUMINOIDS.

The animal skeleton—horns, bones, cartilage, connective tissue, etc., contain nitrogenous compounds which are converted by boiling into substances that form with water a jelly-like mass. These are known as the gelatins.

Collagen.

The chief constituent of the connective tissues is *collagen*. This is insoluble in cold water, but in hot water becomes soluble and yields gelatine. Collagen swells when heated and when treated with dilute acids. Steak increases in bulk when placed over the coals, and tough meat is rendered tender by soaking in vinegar. Freshly killed meat is tough, for the collagen is dry and hard. In time it becomes softened by the acid secretions brought about through bacterial action, and the meat becomes tender and easily masticated. *Tannic acid* has the opposite effect upon collagen, hardening and shrinking it. This effect is taken advantage of in tanning, and is the disadvantage of *boiled* tea as a beverage.

Cooking of Nitrogenous Food-Stuffs.

Cooking should render nitrogenous food more soluble because here, as in every case, digestibility means solubility. Therefore, when the white of

COOKING AND CLEANING. 51

egg (albumin), the curd of milk (casein), or the gluten of wheat are hardened by heat, a much longer time is required to effect solution.

As previously stated, egg albumin is tender and jelly-like when heated from 160 degrees to 180 degrees. This fact should never be forgotten in the cooking of eggs. Raw eggs are easily digested and are rich in nutrition; when heated just enough to coagulate the albumin or "the white," their digestibility is not materially lessened; but when *boiled* the albumin is rendered more difficultly soluble.

Eggs.

To secure the greatest digestibility in combination with palatibility, they may be put into boiling water, placed where the temperature can be kept below 180 degrees, and left from ten to fifteen minutes, or even longer, as the albumin will not harden and the yolk will become mealy.

To fry eggs the fat must reach a temperature— 300 degrees or over—far above that at which the albumin of the egg becomes tough, hard, and well-nigh insoluble.

The oyster, though not rich in nutrition, is readily digested when raw or slightly warmed. When fried in a batter, it is so protected by the water in the dough that the heat does not rise high enough to render insoluble the albuminous morsel within. Frying in crumbs (in which there is always 30 to 40

Oysters.

per cent water, even though the bread be dry) is another though less efficient method of protection for the albumin. Corn meal, often used as a coating, contains 10 to 12 per cent of water.

Experiments on the digestibility of gluten have proved that a high temperature largely decreases its solubility. Subjected to artificial digestion for the same length of time, nearly two and one half times as much nitrogen was dissolved from the raw gluten as from that which had been baked.*

When gluten is combined with starch, as in the cereals, the difficulties of correct cooking are many, for the heat which increases the digestibility of the starch decreases that of the gluten.

The same principle applies to *cascin*—the albuminous constituent of milk. There seems to be no doubt that boiling decreases its solubility, and, consequently, its digestibility for persons of delicate digestive power.

The cooking of beans and all leguminous vegetables should soften the cellulose and break up the compact grains of starch. Vegetables should never be cooked in hard water, for the legumin of the vegetable forms an insoluble compound with the lime or magnesia of the water.

In the case of flesh the cooking should soften

---

*The Effect of Heat upon the Digestibility of Gluten, by Ellen H. Richards. A. M., S. B., and Elizabeth Mason, A. B. Technology Quarterly, Vol. vii., 63

COOKING AND CLEANING.

and loosen the connective tissue, so that the little bundles of fibre which contain the nutriment may fall apart easily when brought in contact with the teeth. Any process which toughens and hardens the meat should be avoided.

Whenever it is desired to retain the juices within the meat or fish, it should be placed in boiling water that the albumin of the surface may be hardened and so prevent the escape of the albumin of the interior. The temperature should then be lowered and kept between 160 and 180 degrees during the time needed for the complete breaking down of the connective tissues. When the nutriment is to be used in broths, stews or soups, the meat should be placed in cold water, heated very slowly and the temperature not allowed to rise above 180 degrees until the extraction is complete. To dissolve the softened collagen, a temperature of 212 degrees is necessary for a short time.

The object of all cooking is to make the foodstuffs more palatable or more digestible or both combined.

Object of Cooking.

In general, the starchy foods are rendered more digestible by cooking; the albuminous and fatty foods less digestible.

The appetite of civilized man craves and custom encourages the putting together of raw materials of such diverse chemical composition that the processes of cooking are also made complex.

Bread—the staff of life—requires a high degree of heat to kill the plant-life, and long baking to prepare the starch for solution; while, by the same process, the gluten is made less soluble.

Fats, alone, are easily digested, but in the ordinary method of frying, they not only become decomposed themselves, and, therefore, injurious; but they also prevent the necessary action of heat, or of the digestive ferments upon the starchy materials with which the fats are mixed.

Pastry owes its harmful character to this interference of fat with the proper solution of the starch. *Good pastry* requires the intimate mixture of flour with solid fat. The starch granules of the flour must absorb water, swell, and burst before they can be dissolved. The fat does not furnish enough water to accomplish this, and it so coats the starch granules as to prevent the sufficient absorption of water in mixing, or from the saliva during mastication. This coating of fat is not removed till late in the process of digestion. The same effect is produced by the combining of flour and fat in made gravies.

The effect of cooking upon the solubility of the three important food-principals may be broadly stated thus:—

Starchy foods are made more soluble by long cooking at moderate temperatures or by heat high enough to dextrinize a portion of the starch, as in the brown crust of bread.

Nitrogenous foods. The animal and vegetable albumins are made less soluble by heat; the animal albuminoids more soluble.

Fats are readily absorbed in their natural condition, but are decomposed at very high temperatures and their products become irritants.

CHAPTER V.

THE ART OF COOKING.

FLAVORS AND CONDIMENTS.

THE science as well as the art of cooking lies in the production of a subtle something which gives zest to the food and which, though infinitesimal in quantity, is of priceless value. It is the savory potage, the mint, anise and cummin, the tasteful morsel, the appetizing odor, which is, rightly, the pride of the cook's heart.

The most general term for this class of stimulating substances is, perhaps, flavor—the *gout* of the French, the *Genuss-Mittel* (enjoyment-giver) of the Germans.

The development of this quality in food—taste, savor, relish, flavor or what not, which makes "the mouth water," depends, in every case, upon chemical changes more subtle than any others known to us. The change in the coffee berry by roasting is a familiar illustration. The heat of the fire causes the breaking up of a substance existing in the berry and the production of several new ones. If the heat is not sufficient, the right odor will not be given; if it is too great, the aroma will be dissipated into the air or the compound will be destroyed.

This is an excellent illustration of the narrow margin along which success lies. It is also chemically typical of the largest number of flavors, which seem to be of the nature of oils, set free by the breaking up of the complex substances of which they form a part. Nature has prepared these essential oils by the heat of the sun. They give the taste to green vegetables; while in fruits they are present with certain acids, and both together cause the pleasure-giving and therapeutic effects for which fruit is noted.

Nature of Flavors.

It is probable that the flavors of roasted corn, well-cooked oatmeal, toasted bread, also belong to this class. Broiled steak and roasted turkey are also illustrations, and with coffee show how easily the mark is overstepped—a few seconds too long, a very few degrees too hot, and the delicate morsel becomes an acrid, irritating mass.

From this standpoint, cooking is an art as exact as the pharmacist's, and the person exercising it should receive as careful preparation; for these flavors, which are so highly prized, are many of them the drugs and poisons of the apothecary and are to be used with as much care. This is an additional reason for producing them by legitimate means from the food itself, and not by adding the crude materials in quantities relatively enormous to those of the food substances.

Chemistry of Flavors.
The chemistry of cooking is therefore largely the chemistry of flavor-production—the application of heat to the food material in such a way as to bring about the right changes and *only* these.

The flavors produced by cooking, correctly done, will be delicate and unobtrusive. Usually, except for broiled meats, a low heat applied for a long time, with the use of closed cooking vessels, develops the best flavors; while quick cooking, which necessitates a high temperature, robs the fine products of nature's laboratory of their choicest elements. Present American cookery, especially, sins in this respect. Either the food is insipid from lack of flavor or crudely seasoned at the last moment.

The secret of the success of our grandmothers' cooking lay not solely in the brick oven—in the low, steady heat it furnished—but in the care, thought, and infinite pains they put into the preparation of their simple foods. Compared with these, the "one-minute" cereals, the "lightning" pudding mixtures of the present are insipid, or tasteless. Experience with the Aladdin Oven is an education in flavor production.

Condiments and their Effect.
Another source of stimulating flavor is found in the addition of various substances called Condiments. These consist of materials, of whatever

nature, added to the food compounds, to give them a relish. Their use is legitimate; their abuse, harmful. The effect of flavors is due to the stimulation of the nerves of taste and smell. Condiments should be used in a way to cause a like stimulation of the nerves. If they are added to food materials before or during the cooking process, a small quantity imparts a flavor to the entire mixture. If added to the cooked food, a larger quantity is used and the effect lasts, not only while the food is in contact with the nerves of the mouth, but also throughout the digestive tract, causing an irritation of the mucous membranes themselves. The tissues become weakened, and, in time, lose the power of normal action.

Cayenne pepper directly applied to the food, although sometimes a help, is oftener the cause in dyspepsia. Highly seasoned food tends to weaken the digestion in the end, by calling for more secretion than is needed and so tiring out, as it were, the glands. It is like the too frequent and violent application of the whip to a willing steed—by and by he learns to disregard it. Just enough to accomplish the purpose is nature's economy.

This economy is quick to recognize and be satisfied with a food which is easily digested without impairing the functional powers of the digestive fluids. A child seldom shows a desire for condiments unless these have been first unwisely added by adults. *Flavors* are largely odors, or odors and tastes combined, and act upon the nervous system in a natural way. *Condiments*, in many cases, are powerful, stimulating drugs, exciting the inner linings of the stomach to an increased and abnormal activity. Medicinally they may act as tonics. The skill of the cook consists in steering between the two digestion possibilities—hinder and help.

Stimulants. Some relish-giving substances, as meat extracts, the caffeine of coffee, theine of tea, theo-bromine of cocoa, and alcohol of wines go directly into the blood and here act upon the nervous system. They quicken the circulation and, therefore, stimulate to increased activity. The cup of coffee thus drives out the feeling of lassitude from wearied nerves and muscles. Wine should never be treated as an article of diet, but as a *Genuss-Mittel*.

Cooking of Vegetables. The secret of the cooking of vegetables is the judicious production of flavor. In this the French cook excels. She adds a little meat juice to the cooked vegetables, thus obtaining the desired flavor with the cheaper nutritious food. This wise use of meats for flavor, while the actual food value is made up from the vegetable kingdom, is an important item in public kitchens, institutions, or wherever expense must be closely calculated.

Economy in Cooking. In the study of economy, flavor-creation is of the

COOKING AND CLEANING.   61

utmost importance. In foods, as everywhere, science and art must supplement the purse, making the few and cheaper materials necessary for nutrition into a variety of savory dishes. Without the appetizing flavor, many a combination of food materials is utterly worthless, for this alone stimulates the desire or appetite, the absence of which may prevent digestion. Food which pleases the palate, unless this has been abnormally educated, is usually wholesome, and judgment based on flavor is normally a sound one.

Starch may be cooked according to the most approved methods; but, if there is no saliva, the starch is without food value. The piece of meat may be done to a turn; but, if there is no gastric juice in the stomach, it will not be dissolved, and hence is useless. A homely illustration will best serve our turn,—a cow may retain her milk by force of will. It is well known how much a contented mind has to do with her readiness to give milk and the quantity of milk she will yield. The various glands of the human body seem to have a like action. The dry mouth fails to moisten the food, and the stimulating flavor is lost. On the other hand the mouth "waters," and food is soon digested. The cow may be utterly foolish and whimsical in her ideas—so may persons. There may not be the least reason

Conditions for Digestion.

THE CHEMISTRY OF

why a person should turn away from a given food, but if he does——? He suffers for his whims.

Serving

Hence the cook's art is most important, for its results must often overcome adverse mental conditions by nerve-stimulating flavors. The art of serving, though out of place here, should be attentively studied with the effect on the appetite especially in view. This is of the utmost importance in connection with hospital cooking.

Discretion in Cooking.

Specific flavors, though agreeable in themselves, should be used with discretion. In Norway, the salmon is designedly cooked so as not to retain much of its characteristic savor, for this is too decided a flavor for an article of daily diet. In soups and stews a "bouquet" of flavors is better than the prominence of any one, although certain favorite dishes may have a constant flavor.

Bacterial Action Produces Flavors.

Nature has produced many flavors and guarded well the secret of their production; but science is fast discovering their sources, as bacterial life and action are better understood. Now, the "June flavor" of butter may be produced in December, by inoculating milk with the right "butter bacillus."

Cooking an Art.

Cooking has thus become an art worthy the attention of intelligent and learned women. The laws of chemical action are founded upon the laws of definite proportions, and whatever is added more

COOKING AND CLEANING.

than enough, is in the way. The head of every household should study the condition of her family, and tempt them with dainty dishes, if that is what they need. Let her see to it that no burst of ill temper, no sullen disposition, no intemperance of any kind be caused by *her ignorance* or *her disregard* of the chemical laws governing the reactions of the food she furnishes.

When this science and this art takes its place beside the other sciences and other arts, one crying need of the world will be satisfied.

We have now considered the three classes of food in one or more of which all staple articles of diet may be placed—the carbohydrates (starch and sugar), the fats and the nitrogenous material. Some general principles of diet, indicated by science, remain to be discussed.

Diet.

All preparation of food-stuffs necessary to make them into suitable food for man comes under the head of what has been called *"external digestion."* The processes of *internal digestion* begin in the mouth. Here the saliva not only lubricates the finely divided portions of the food materials, but, in the case of starch, begins the process of changing the insoluble starch into a soluble sugar. This process is renewed in the small intestine. The fats

<small>Processes of Digestion. Saliva.</small>

are emulsified in the small intestine, and, with the soluble carbohydrates, are here largely absorbed.

All the chemical changes which the nitrogenous food stuffs undergo are not well understood. Such food should be finely comminuted in the mouth, because, as before stated, chemical action is rapid in proportion to the fineness of division; but it is in the stomach that the first chemical change occurs.

The chief agents of this change are pepsin and related substances, aided by the acid of the gastric juice; these together render the nitrogenous substance soluble and capable of passing through the membranes. Neither seems able to do this alone, for if the acid is neutralized, action ceases; and if pepsin is absent, digestion does not take place.

Decompositions of a very complex kind occur, *peptones* are formed which are soluble compounds, and the nitrogen finally passes out of the system as *urea*, being separated by the kidneys, as carbon dioxide is separated by the lungs.

One of the most obvious questions is: Which is best for human food—starch or fat, beans and peas, or flesh? As to starch or fat, the question has been answered by experience, and science has only tried to explain the reason. The colder the climate, the more fat the people eat. The tropical nations live

COOKING AND CLEANING.

chiefly on starchy foods, as rice. From previous statements it will be seen that this is right in principle. Fat yields more heat than rice; therefore the inference is plain that in the cold of winter fat is appropriate food, while in the heat of summer rice or some other starchy food should be substituted.

Seasonable Diet. The diet of summer should also contain much fruit. Increased perspiration makes necessary an increased supply of water. This may be furnished largely by fruits, and with the water certain acids are taken which act as correctives in the digestive processes.

No evident rule can be seen in the case of the albuminous foods. At most, the class can be divided into three groups. The first includes the material of vegetable origin, as peas, lentils, and the gluten of wheat. The second comprises the white of egg and the curd of milk—material of animal origin. The third takes in all the animal flesh used by mankind as food.

Economy of a Mixed Diet. Considering the question from a purely chemical standpoint, without regarding the moral or social aspects of the case, two views stand out clearly: 1st. If the stored-up vegetable matter has required the force derived from the sun to prepare it, the tearing apart and giving back to the air and earth the elements of which it was built up will yield the same amount of force to whatever tears it down;

but a certain amount of energy must be used up in this destruction. 2d. If the animal, having accomplished the decomposition of the vegetable and appropriated the material, is killed, and the prepared nitrogenous food in the form of muscle is eaten by man, then little force is necessary to render the food assimilable; it is only to be dissolved in order that it may enter into the circulation. The force-producing power is not lost; it is only transferred to another animal body. Hence the ox or the sheep can do a part of man's work for him in preparing the vegetable food for use, and man may thus accomplish more than he otherwise could. This digestion of material outside of the body is carried still further, by man, in the manufacture of partially digested foods,—"malted," "peptonized," "pre-digested," etc. Exclusive use of these is fraught with danger, for the organs of digestion lose power, if that which they have, however little, be long unused.

Food of Young Animals. Nearly all, if not all, young animals live on food of animal origin. The young of the human race live on milk; but it has been found by experience that milk is not the best food for the adult to live upon to the exclusion of all else. It is not conducive to quickness of thought or general bodily activity.

Need of Vegetable Food. Experience leads to the conclusion that mankind needs some vegetable food. Two facts sustain this inference. The digestive organs of the herbivorous animals form fifteen to twenty per cent of the whole weight of the body. Those of the carnivorous animals form five to six per cent, those of the human race, about eight per cent. The length of the canal through which the food passes varies in about the same ratio in the three classes. A mixed diet seems to be indicated as desirable by every test which has been applied; but the proportions in which the vegetable and animal food are to be mingled, as well as the relative quantities of carbonaceous and nitrogenous material which will give the best efficiency to the human machine are not so easily determined.

Nature seems to have made provision for the excess of heat resulting from the oxidation of too much starch or fat, by the ready means of evaporation of water from the surface; this loss of water being supplied by drinking a fresh supply, which goes, without change, into the circulation. The greater the heat, the greater the evaporation; hence the importance of water as an article of diet, especially for children, must not be overlooked. For an active person, the supply has been estimated at three quarts per day. Water is the heat regulator of the animal body. An article entitled "Water

Water and Air as Food.

and Air as Food,"* by one of the authors of this book, treats this subject more thoroughly.

While dangerous disease seldom results from eating an excess of starch or fat, because the portion not wanted is rejected as if it were so much sand, many of the most complicated disorders do result from an excess of nitrogenous diet.

The readiness with which such substances undergo putrefaction, and the many noxious products to which such changes give rise, should lead us to be more careful as to the quantity of this food.

From experiments made by the best investigators, it seems probable that only one third of the estimated daily supply of food is available for kinetic force; that is, that only about one third of the total energy contained in the daily food can be utilized in digging trenches, carrying bricks, climbing mountains, designing bridges, or writing poems and essays. The other two thirds is used up in the internal work of the body—the action of the heart, lungs, and the production of the large amount of heat necessary to life.

It has been estimated that a *growing* person needs about one part of nitrogenous food to four of starch and fat; a *grown* person, one part nitrogenous to five or six of starch and fat. If this is

---

* Rumford Kitchen Leaflet, No. 6, *American Kitchen Magazine*, Vol. IV., 257.

COOKING AND CLEANING.

true, then we may make out a life ration, or that amount of food which is necessary to keep the human machine in existence.

For this climate, and for the habits of our people, we have estimated this life ration as approximately:

Proteid.	Fat.	Carbohydrates.	Calories.
75 grams.	40 grams.	325 grams.	2,000.

The amount of energy given out in the form of work cannot exceed the amount of energy taken in in the form of food; so this life ration is increased to make a maximum and minimum for a work ration. For professional or literary persons the following may be considered a sufficient maximum and minimum:

Proteid.	Fat.	Carbohydrates.	Calories.
125 grams.	125 grams.	450 grams.	3,500.
110 grams.	90 grams.	420 grams.	3,000.

For hard manual labor about one-third is to be added to the above rations. An examination of the actual dietaries of some of the very poor who eat just enough to live, without doing any work, shows that in twelve cases the average diet was:

Proteid.	Fat.	Carbohydrates.	Calories.
31 grams.	81 grams.	272 grams.	2,257.

For further information on these points see the list of works at the end of this book.

The first office of the food, then, is to keep the human body in a high condition of health; the second, to enable it to exert force in doing the work

Offices of Food.

of the world; and a third, the value of which it is hardly possible to estimate, is to furnish an important factor in the restoration of the body to normal condition, when health is lost. In sickness, far more than in health, a knowledge of the right proportions of the essential food substances, and of the absolute quantity or food value given, is important. How many a life has been lost because of a lack of this knowledge the world will never know.

PART II.

THE CHEMISTRY OF CLEANING.

CHAPTER I.

Dust.

MANY a housewife looks upon dust as her inveterate enemy against whom incessant warfare brings only visible defeat. Between the battles, let us study the enemy — the composition of his forces, his tactics, his ammunition, in order that we may find a vantage ground from which to direct our assault, or from which we may determine whether it is really an enemy which we are fighting.

The Century dictionary defines dust as "Earth, or other matter in fine dry particles so attenuated that they can be raised and carried by the wind." This suggests that dust is no modern product of the universe. Indeed, its ancestry is hidden in those ages of mystery before man was. Who can say that it does not reach to that eternity which can be designated only by "In the beginning?" *Definition of Dust.*

Necessity of Dust.

Tyndall proved by delicate experiments that when all dust was removed from the track of a beam of light, *there* was darkness. So before the command "Let there be light," the dust-condition of light must have been present. Balloonists find that the higher they ascend the deeper the color of the sky. When at a distance of some miles, the sky is nearly black, there is so little dust to scatter the rays of light. If the stellar spaces are dustless, they must be black and, therefore, colorless. The moisture of the air collects about the dust-particles giving us clouds and, with them, all the glories of sunrise and sunset. Fogs, too, are considered to be masses of "water-dust," and ships far out at sea have had their sails colored by this dust, while sailing through banks of fog. Thinking, now, of the above definition, it may be said that the earth, in its final analysis, must be dust deposited during past ages; that to dust is due the light necessary to life, and that without it certain phenomena of nature—clouds, color, fog, perhaps, even rain and snow could not exist.

It behooves us, then, as inhabitants of this dust-formed and dust-beautified earth to speak well of our habitation. We have found no enemy yet. The enemy must be lurking in the "other matter." This the dictionary says is in powdered form, carried by the air, and, therefore, at times existent in

COOKING AND CLEANING. 73

it, as has been seen. A March wind gives sensible proof of this, but what about the quiet air, whether out of doors or in our houses?

An old writer has said: "The sun discovers *atomes*, though they be invisible by candle-light, and makes them dance naked in his beams." Those sensible particles with these "*atomes*," which become visible in the track of a beam of light whenever it enters a darkened room, make up the dust whose character is to be studied.

<small>Visible and Invisible Dust.</small>

Astronomers find meteoric dust in the atmosphere. When this falls on the snow and ice fields of the Arctic regions, it is readily recognized. The eruption of Krakátoa proved that volcanic dust is disseminated world-wide. Dust contains mineral matter, also, from the wear and tear of nature's forces upon the rocks, bits of dead matter given off by animal and vegetable organisms, minute fibres from clothing, the pollen of plants, the dry and pulverized excrement of animals. These constituents are easily detected—are they all?

<small>Composition of Dust</small>

Let a mixture of flour and water stand out-of-doors, leave a piece of bread or bit of cheese on the pantry shelves for a week. The mixture ferments, the bread and cheese mold. Formerly, these changes were attributed to the "access of air"—i. e., to the action upon the substances, of the oxygen of the air; later experiments have proved that if the

<small>Dust Plants.</small>

air be previously passed through a cotton-wool filter it will cause no change in the mixture. The oxygen is not filtered out, so *it* cannot be the cause of the fermentation. Now, all the phenomena of fermentation are known to be caused by minute vegetable organisms which exist everywhere in the air and settle from it when it becomes dry and still. They are molds, yeasts and bacteria. All are microscopic and many sub-microscopic. They are found wherever the atmosphere extends—some feet below the surface of the ground and some miles above it, although on the tops of the highest mountains and, perhaps, far out at sea, the air is practically free from earthly dust, and therefore nearly free from these forms. The volcanic dust of the upper air does not appear to contain them. They are all spoken of as "germs," because they are capable of developing into growing forms. All are plants belonging to the fungi; in their manner of life essentially like the plants we cherish, requiring food, growing, and reproducing their kind. They require moisture in order to grow or multiply; but, like the seeds of higher plants, can take on a condition calculated to resist hard times and endure these for long periods; then when moisture is furnished, they immediately spring into growth. In the bacteria these spores are simply a resting stage and are not reproduc-

COOKING AND CLEANING. 75

tive; while, in molds, they bring forth an active, growing plant.

The common puff-ball (*Lycoperdon*), the "smoke" ball of the country child, well illustrates both vegetative and spore stages. This belongs to the fungi, is closely related to the molds, and consists of a spherical outer wall of two layers, enclosing tissues which form numerous chambers with membraneous partitions. Within these chambers are formed the reproductive cells or spores. When ripe, the mass becomes dry, the outer layer of the wall scales off, the inner layer splits open, allowing the minute dry spores to escape as a "cloud of dust." These are readily carried by the wind until caught on some moist spot favorable for their growth. They are found on dry, sandy soils, showing that very little moisture is needed; but when this is found, the spore swells, germinates, and grows into a new vegetative ball, which completes the cycle. *Spores.*

Wheat grains taken from the wrappings of mummies are said to have sprouted when given moisture and warmth. Whether this be true or not, there can be no doubt that the vitality of some seeds and spores is wonderfully enduring. *Vita Endurance.*

The spores of some of the bacteria may be boiled and many may be frozen—still life will remain.

Aristotle declared that "all dry bodies become damp and all damp bodies which are dried engen- *Dangerous Dust.*

der animal life." He believed these dust germs to be animalcules spontaneously generated wherever the conditions were favorable. How could he, without the microscope, explain in any other way the sudden appearance of such myriads of living forms?

Now, it is recognized that the air everywhere contains the spores of molds and bacteria, and it is this dust carried in the air which falls in our houses. *This* is our enemy.

A simple housemaid once said that the sun brought in the dust "atomes" through the window, and the careful, old, New England housewife thought the same. So, she shut up the best room, making it dark and, therefore, damp. Unwittingly, she furnished to them the most favorable conditions of growth, in which they might increase at the rate of many thousands in twenty-four hours.

"Let there be light" must be the ever-repeated command, if we would take the first outpost of the enemy.

We live in an invisible atmosphere of dust, we are constantly adding to this atmosphere by the processes of our own growth and waste, and, finally, we shall go the way of all the earth, contributing our bodies to the making of more dust. Thus dust has a decided two-fold aspect of friendliness and enmity. We have no wish to guard ourselves against friends; so, for the present purposes, the

COOKING AND CLEANING.

inimical action of dust, as affecting the life and health of man, alone need challenge our attention. The mineral dust, animal waste, or vegetable debris, however irritating to our membranes, or destructive of our clothing, are enemies of minor importance, compared with these myriads of living germs, which we feel not, hear not, see not, and know not until they have done their work.

From a sanitary point of view, the most important of the three living ingredients of dust is that called bacteria. They are the most numerous, the most widely distributed, and perhaps the smallest of all living things. Their natural home is the soil. Here they are held by moisture, and by the gelatinous character caused, in large part, by their own vital action. When the surface of the ground becomes dry, they are carried from it, by the wind, into the air. Rain and snow wash them down; running streams take them from the soil; so that, at all times, the natural waters contain immense numbers of them. They are heavier than the air and settle from it in an hour or two, when it is dry and still. They are now quietly resting on this page which you are reading. They are on the floor, the tops of doors and windows, the picture frames, in every bit of "fluff" which so adroitly eludes the broom—in fact, everywhere where dust can lodge.

The second ingredient, in point of numbers, is

Bacteria.

Molds.

the molds. They, too, are present in the air, both outside and inside of our houses; but being much lighter than the bacteria, they do not settle so quickly, and are much more readily carried into the air again, by a very slight breeze.

Yeasts. The third, or wild yeasts, are not usually troublesome in the air or in the dust of the house, where ordinary cleanliness rules.

"Dirt." To the bacteriologist, then, everything is dirty unless the conditions for germ-growth have been removed, and the germs, once present, killed. All of this dirt cannot be said to be "matter in the wrong place," only when it is the wrong kind of matter in some particular place. The bacteria are Nature's scavengers. Every tree that falls in the forest—animal or vegetable matter of all kinds is immediately attacked by these ever-present, invisible agents. By their life-processes, absorbing, secreting, growing and reproducing, they silently convert such matter into various harmless substances. They are faithful laborers, earning an honest living, taking their wages as they go. Their number and omnipresence show the great amount of work there must be for them to do.

Then why should we enter the lists against such opponents? Because this germ-community is like any other typical community.

The majority of the individuals are law-abiding,

COOKING AND CLEANING.

respectable citizens; yet in some dark corner a thief may hide, or a cut-throat steal in unawares. If this happens, property may be destroyed and life itself endangered.

Molds, and some of the yeasts, destroy our property; but a certain few of the bacteria cause disease and death. In a very real sense, so soon as an organism begins to live it begins to die; but these are natural processes and do not attract attention so long as the balance between the two is preserved. When the vital force is lessened, by whatever cause, disease eventually shows itself. Methods for the *cure* of disease are as old as disease itself; but methods for the *prevention* of disease are of late birth. Here and there along the past, some minds, wiser than their age, have seen the possibilities of such prevention; but superstition and ignorance have long delayed the fruition of their hopes.

"An ounce of prevention is worth a pound of cure," though oft repeated has borne scanty fruit in daily living. When the cause of smallpox, tuberculosis, diphtheria, typhoid fever, and other infectious diseases is known to be a living plant, which cannot live without food, it seems, at first sight, a simple matter to starve it out of existence. This has proved to be no simple nor easy task; so much the more is each person bound by the law of self-love and the greater law, "Thou shalt love

Prevention of Disease.

thy neighbor as thyself," to do his part toward driving these diseases from the world.

Any one of these dust-germs is harmless so long as it cannot grow. Prevent their growth in the human body, and the diseased condition cannot occur.

Prevention, then, is the watchword of modern sanitary science.

It may be asked: How do the germs cause disease?

Why do they not *always* cause disease?

Numerous answers have been given during the short time the germ theory of infectious diseases has been studied. If we follow the history of this study, we may find, at least, a partial answer.

Action of Bacteria.

A person is "attacked" by smallpox, diphtheria, lockjaw, typhoid fever, or some kindred disease. Common speech recognizes in the use of the word "attacked" that an enemy from outside has begun, by force, a violent onset upon the person. This enemy—a particular bacterium or other germ, has entered the body in some way. There may have been contact with another person ill with the same disease. The germ may have entered through food on which it was resting, by water, or by air as it touched the exposed flesh, where the skin was broken by a scratch or cut. It found in the blood or flesh the moisture and warmth necessary for its

COOKING AND CLEANING. 81

growth, and, probably, a supply of food at once desirable and bountiful. It began to feed, to grow, and to multiply rapidly, until the little one became a million. At this stage the patient knew he was ill. It was thoughf, at first, that the mere presence in the body of such enormous numbers caused the disease.

Bacteria like the same kinds of food which we like. Though they can and will live on starvation rations, they prefer a more luxurious diet. This fact led to the idea that they supplied their larder by stealing from the food supply of the invaded body; so that, while the uninvited and unwelcome guest dined luxuriously, the host sickened of starvation. This answer is now rejected. *(Food of Bacteria.)*

The food of the bacteria is not only similar in kind to our own food, but it must also undergo like processes of solution and absorption.

Solution is brought about by the excretion of certain substances, similar in character and in action to the ferments secreted in the animal mouth, stomach and intestines. These excretions reduce the food materials to liquids, which are then absorbed.

The pathogenic or disease-producing germs are found to throw out during their processes of assimilation and growth, various substances which are poisons to the animal body, as are aconite and digitalis. These are absorbed and carried by the blood throughout the entire system. These poisons are called toxines. It is now believed that it is these bacterial products, the toxines or poisons, which are the immediate cause of the diseased condition.

Inoculation. Inoculation of some of the lower animals with the poisoned blood of a diseased person, in which blood no germ itself was present, has repeatedly produced the identical disease. It is far easier to keep such manufacturers out of the body than to "regulate" their manufactures after an entrance has been gained.

These faint glimpses into the "Philosophy of Cleanness" lead to another question, namely: How shall we keep clean?

Requisites or Cleanness. The first requisite for cleanness is light—direct sunlight if possible. It not only reveals the visible dirt, but allies itself with us as an active agent towards the destruction of the invisible elements of uncleanness. That which costs little or nothing is seldom appreciated; so this all-abundant, freely-given light is often shut out through man's greed or through mistaken economy. The country dweller surrounds his house with evergreens or shade trees, the city dweller is surrounded by high brick walls. Blinds, shades, or thick draperies shut out still more, and prevent the beneficent sunlight from acting its rôle of germ-prevention and germ-de-

Sunlight.

struction. Bright-colored carpets and pale-faced children are the opposite results which follow. "Sunshine is the enemy of disease, which thrives in darkness and shadow." Consumption and scrofulous diseases are well-nigh inevitable, when blinds are tightly closed and trees surround the house, causing darkness, and, thereby, inviting dampness. As far as possible let the exterior of the house be bathed in sunlight. Then let it enter every nook and cranny. It will dry up the moisture, without which the tiny disease germs or other plants cannot grow; it will find and rout them by its chemical action. Its necessity and power in moral cleanness, who can measure?

More plentiful than sunlight is air. We cannot shut it out entirely as we can light; but there is dirty air just as truly as dirty clothes and dirty water. The second requisite for cleanness, then, is *pure air*. Pure Air.

Primitive conditions of human life required no thought of the air supply, for man lived in the open; but civilization brings the need of attention and care for details; improvements in some directions are balanced by disadvantages in others; luxuries crowd out necessities, and man pays the penalty for his disregard of Nature's laws. Sunlight, pure air and pure water are our common birthright, which we often bargain away for so-called comforts. Primitive Conditions of Life.

Sunlight is purity itself. Man cannot contaminate it, but the air about him is what man makes it. Naturally, air is the great "disinfectant, antiseptic and purifier, and not to be compared for a moment with any of artificial contrivance," but under man's abuse it may become a death-dealing breath.

Charlemagne said: "Right action is better than knowledge; but to act right one must know right." Nature's supply of pure air is sufficient for all, but to have it always in its pure state requires knowledge and constant, intelligent action.

Products of Combustion. The gaseous products of the combustion carried on within our bodies; like products from our artificial sources of heat and light—burning coal, gas and oil; waste matters of life and manufactures carried into the air through fermentation and putrefaction—all these, with the innumerable sources of dust we have already found, load the air with impurities. Some are quickly recognized by sight, smell or taste; but many, and these the more dangerous, are unrecognizable by any sense. They show their actions in our weakened, diseased and useless bodies. Dr. James Johnson says: "All the deaths resulting from fevers are but a drop in the ocean, when compared with the numbers who perish from bad air."

Air Pollution. The per cent of pollution in the country is much smaller than in the city, where a crowded popula-

COOKING AND CLEANING. 85

tion and extensive manufactories are constantly pouring forth impure matters, but by rapidly moving currents, even this large per cent is soon diluted and carried away. Would that the air in country *houses*, during both winter and summer, might show an equally small per cent!

Air is a real substance. It can be weighed. It will expand, and may be compressed like other gases. It requires considerable force to move it, and this force varies with the temperature. When a bottle is full of air, no more can be poured in. Our houses are full of air all the time. No more can come in till some has gone out. In breathing, we use up a little, but it is immediately replaced by expired air, which is impure. Were there no exits for this air, no pure air could enter, and we should soon die of slow suffocation. The better built the house the quicker the suffocation, unless special provision be made for a current of fresh air to push out the bad. Fortunately no house is air tight. Air will come in round doors and windows, but this is neither sufficient to drive out the bad nor to dilute it beyond harm. Therefore the air of all rooms must be often and completely changed, either by special systems of ventilation, or by intelligent action in the opening of doors and windows. Air a Substance.

Sunlight and pure air are the silent but powerful Aids in Cleanness.

allies of the housewife in her daily struggle toward the ideal cleanness, i. e., sanitary cleanness, the cleanness of health. Without these allies she may spend her strength for naught, for the plant-life of the quiet, dust-laden air will grow and multiply far beyond her powers of destruction. With these allies the victory over uncleanness might be easy and sure were dust *alone* the enemy to be fought; but the mixture of dust with greasy, sugary, or smoky deposits makes the struggle twofold.

CHAPTER II.

Dust Mixtures.

Grease and Dust.

THE various processes of housework give rise to many volatile substances. These, the vapors of water or fat, if not carried out of the house in their vaporous state will cool and settle upon all exposed surfaces, whether walls, furniture or fabrics. This thin film entangles and holds the dust, clouding and soiling, with a layer more or less visible, everything within the house. Imperfect ventilation allows additional deposits from fires and lights—the smoky products of incomplete combustion. *Sources of Dirt.*

Thorough ventilation is, then, a preventive measure, which ensures a larger removal not only of the volatile matters, but also of the dust, with its possible disease germs.

Dust, *alone*, might be removed from most surfaces with a damp or even with a dry cloth, or from fabrics by vigorous shaking or brushing; but, usually, the greasy or sugary deposits must first be broken up and, thus, the dust set free. This must be accomplished without harm to the material upon *Removal of Dust.*

which the unclean deposit rests. Here is a broad field for the application of chemical knowledge.

Processes of Cleaning. Cleaning, then, involves two processes: First, the greasy film must be broken up, that the entangled dust may be set free. Second, the dust must be removed by mechanical means. Disinfection sometimes precedes the second process, in order that the dangerous dust-plants may be killed before removal.

To understand the methods of dust removal, it is necessary to consider the chemical character of the grease and, also, that of the materials effectual in acting upon it.

Grease–Oils. Grease or fats, called oils when liquid at ordinary temperature, are chemical compounds made of different elements, but all containing an ingredient known to the chemist as a fatty acid.

The chemist finds in nature certain elements which, with the fatty acids, form compounds entirely different in character from either of the original ingredients. These elements are called the alkali metals and the neutral compounds formed by their union with the acid of the fat are familiarly known to the chemist as salts.

Alkali Metals. The chemical group of "alkali metals" comprises six substances: Ammonium, Cæsium, Lithium, Potassium, Rubidium and Sodium. Two of the six—Cæsium and Rubidium—were discovered by means

COOKING AND CLEANING.

of the spectroscope, not many years ago, in the mineral waters of Dürckheim, and, probably, the total amount for sale of all the salts of these two metals could be carried in one's pocket. A third alkali metal—Lithium—occurs in several minerals, and its salts are of frequent use in the laboratory, but it is not sufficiently abundant to be of commercial importance. As regards the three remaining alkali metals, the hydrate of Ammonium $(NH_4)OH$, is known as "Volatile Alkali," the hydrates of Potassium, KOH, and Sodium, $NaOH$, as "Caustic Alkalies." With these three alkalies and their compounds, and these alone, are we concerned in housekeeping. The volatile alkali, Ammonia, is now prepared in quantity and price such that every housekeeper may become acquainted with its use. It does not often occur in soaps, but it is valuable for use in all cleansing operations—the kitchen, the laundry, the bath, the washing of woolens, and in other cases where its property of evaporation, without leaving any residue to attack the fabric or to attract anything from the air, is invaluable. The most extensive household use of the alkalies is in the laundry, under which head they will be more specifically described.

Some of the fatty acids combine readily with alkalies to form compounds which we call *soaps*. Others in contact with the alkalies form emulsions,

Soaps.

so-called, in which the fatty globules are suspended, forming an opaque liquid. These emulsions are capable of being indefinitely diluted with clear water, and, by this means, the fatty globules are all carried away. Most of the fats are soluble in benzine, ether, chloroform, naphtha or alcohol.

The Problem of Cleaning. If the housekeeper's problem were the simple one of removing the grease alone, she would solve it by the free use of one of these solvents or by some of the strong alkalies. This is what the painter does when he is called to repaint or to refinish; but the housewife wishes to *preserve* the finish or the fabric while she removes the dirt. She must, then, choose those materials which will dissolve or unite with the grease without injury to the articles cleaned.

Cleaning of Different Materials. The greasy film which entangles the unclean and possibly dangerous dust-germs and dust-particles is deposited on materials of widely different character. These materials may be roughly divided into two classes: One, where, on account of some artificial preparation, the uncleanness does not penetrate the material but remains upon the surface, as on wood, metal, minerals, leather and some wall paper; the other, where the grease and dust settle among the fibres, as in fabrics.

"Finish" of Woods. In the interior of the house, woods are seldom used in their natural state. The surface is covered

COOKING AND CLEANING.

with two or more coatings of different substances which add to the wood durability or beauty. The finish used is governed by the character of the wood, the position and the purpose which it serves. The cleaning processes should affect the final coat of finish alone.

Soft woods are finished with paint, stain, oil, shellac, varnish, or with two or more of these combined; hard woods with any of these and, in addition, encaustics of wax, or wax with turpentine or oil.

All these surfaces, except those finished with wax, may be cleaned with a weak solution of soap or ammonia, but the continued use of any such alkali will impair and finally remove the polish. Waxed surfaces are turned dark by water. Finished surfaces should never be scoured nor cleaned with strong alkalies, like sal-soda or potash soaps. To avoid the disastrous effects of these alkalies the solvents of grease may be used or slight friction applied. *Varnish, Oil, Wax.*

Kerosene and turpentine are efficient solvents for grease and a few drops of these on a soft cloth may be used to clean all polished surfaces. The latter cleans the more perfectly and evaporates readily; the former is cheaper, safer, because its vapor is not so inflammable as that of turpentine, and it polishes a little while it cleans; but it evaporates so slowly *Solvents of Grease.*

that the surface must be rubbed dry each time, or dust will be collected and retained. The harder the rubbing, the higher the polish.

Outside of the kitchen, the woodwork of the house seldom needs scrubbing. The greasy layer is readily dissolved by weak alkaline solutions, by kerosene or turpentine, while the imbedded dust is wiped away by the cloth. Polished surfaces keep clean longest. Strong alkalies will eat through the polish by dissolving the oil with which the best paints, stains or polishes are usually mixed. If the finish be removed or broken by deep scratches, the wood itself absorbs the grease and dust, and the stain may have to be scraped out.

Woodwork, whether in floors, standing finish or furniture, from which the dust is carefully wiped every day, will not need frequent cleaning. A few drops of kerosene or some clear oil rubbed on with a second cloth will keep the polish bright and will protect the wood.

Certain preparations of non-drying oils are now in the market, which, when applied to floors, serve to hold the dust and prevent its spreading through the room and settling upon the furnishings. They are useful in school-rooms, stores, etc., where the floor cannot be often cleaned. The dust and dirt stick in the oil and, in time, the whole must be cleaned off and a new coating applied.

Many housewives fear to touch the piano, however clouded or milky the surface may become. The manufacturers say that pianos should be *washed* with soap and water. Use tepid water with a good quality of hard soap and soft woolen or cotton-flannel cloths. Wash a small part at a time, rinse quickly with clear water that the soap may not remain long, and wipe dry immediately. Do all quickly. A well-oiled cloth wiped over the surface and hard rubbing with the hand or with chamois will improve the appearance. If there are deep scratches which go through the polish to the wood, the water and soap should be replaced by rottenstone and oil, or dark lines will appear where the alkali and water touched the natural wood. A Clean Piano.

Painted surfaces, especially if white, may be cleaned with whiting, applied with a moistened woolen cloth or soft sponge. Never let the cloth be wet enough for the water to run or stand in drops on the surface. Wipe "with the grain" of the wood, rinse in clear water with a second soft cloth and wipe dry with a third. All washed surfaces should be wiped dry, for moisture and warmth furnish the favorable conditions of growth for all dust-germs, whether bacteria or molds. Cheese cloth may be used for all polished surfaces, for it neither scratches nor grows linty. Paint.

94   THE CHEMISTRY OF

Walls painted with oil paints may be cleaned with weak ammonia water or whiting in the same manner as woodwork; but if they are tinted with water colors, no cleaning can be done to them, for both liquids and friction will loosen the coloring matter.

Wall-Paper.   Papered walls should be wiped down with cheese cloth, with the rough side of cotton flannel, or some other soft cloth. This will effectually remove all free dust. Make a bag the width of the broom or brush used. Run in drawing strings. Draw the bag over the broom, and tie closely round the handle, just above the broom-corn. Wipe the walls down with a light stroke and the paper will not be injured. An occasional thorough cleansing will be needed to remove the greasy and smoky deposits. The use of bread dough or crumb is not recommended, for organic matter may be left upon the wall. A large piece of aërated rubber—the "sponge" rubber used by artists for erasing their drawings—may be used effectually, and will leave no harmful deposit. "Cartridge" paper may be scoured with fine emery or pumice powder, for the color goes through. Other papers have only a thin layer of color.

Varnished and waxed papers are now made which may be washed with water.

Leather.   Leather may be wiped with a damp cloth or be

kept fresh by the use of a little kerosene. An occasional dressing of some good oil, well rubbed in, will keep it soft and glossy.

Marble may be scoured with fine sand-soap or powdered pumice, or covered with a paste of whiting, borax or pipe-clay, mixed with turpentine, ammonia, alcohol or soft soap. This should be left to dry. When brushed or washed off, the marble will be found clean. Polish with coarse flannel or a piece of an old felt hat. Marble is carbonate of lime, and any acid, even fruit juices, will unite with the lime, driving out the carbon dioxide, which shows itself in effervescence, if the quantity of acid be sufficient. Acids, then, should not touch marble, if it is desired to keep the polish intact. An encaustic of wax and turpentine is sometimes applied to marbles to give them a smooth, shining surface. Marble.

Pastes of whiting, pipe-clay, starch or whitewash may be put over ornaments of alabaster, plaster and the like. The paste absorbs the grease and, by reason of its adhesive character, removes the grime and dust.

Most metals may be washed without harm in a hot alkaline solution or wiped with a little kerosene. Stoves and iron sinks may be scoured with the coarser materials like ashes, emery or pumice; but copper, polished steel, or the soft metals, tin, silver, and zinc require a fine powder that they may not Metals.

be scratched or worn away too rapidly. Metal bathtubs may be kept clean and bright with whiting and ammonia, if rinsed with boiling hot water and wiped dry with soft flannel or chamois.

Porcelain. Porcelain or soapstone may be washed like metal or scoured with any fine material.

Glass. Glass of windows, pictures and mirrors may be cleaned in many ways. It may be covered with a whiting paste mixed with water, ammonia or alcohol. Let the paste remain till dry, when it may be rubbed off with a sponge, woolen cloth or paper. Polish the glass by hard rubbing with newspapers or chamois. Alcohol evaporates more quickly than water and therefore hastens the process; but it is expensive and should not touch the sashes, as it might turn the varnish. Very good results are obtained with a tablespoonful of kerosene to a quart of warm water. In winter, when water would freeze, windows may be wiped with clear kerosene and rubbed dry. Kerosene does not remove fly specks readily, but will take off grease and dust. A bag of coarsely woven cheese-cloth filled with indigo or other powdered blue may be dusted over glass. This, when rubbed hard with soft cloths or chamois, leaves a fine polish.

Success in washing glass depends more upon manipulation than materials. It is largely a matter of patience and polishing. The outer surface of windows often becomes roughened by the dissolving action of rain water, or milky and opaque by action between the sun, rain and the potash or soda in the glass. Ordinary cleaning will not make such windows clear and bright. The opaqueness may sometimes be removed by rubbing thoroughly with dilute muriatic acid. Then polish with whiting.

Household fabrics, whether carpets, draperies or clothing, collect large quantities of dust, which no amount of brushing or shaking will entirely dislodge. They also absorb vapors which condense and hold the dust-germs still more firmly among the fibres. Here the fastness of color and strength of fibre must be considered, for a certain amount of soaking will be necessary in order that the cleansing material may penetrate through the fabric. In general, all fabrics should be washed often in an alkaline solution. If the colors will not stand the application of water, they may be cleansed in naphtha or rubbed with absorbents. The chemistry of dyeing has made such progress during the last ten years that fast colors are more frequently found, even in the cheaper grades of fabrics, than could be possible before this time. It is now more a question of weak fibre than of fleeting color. Heavy fabrics may therefore be allowed to soak for some time in many waters, or portions of naphtha, being rinsed carefully up and down without

<small>Fabrics.</small>

rubbing. All draperies or woolen materials should be carefully beaten and brushed before any other cleaning is attempted. Wool fabrics hold much of the dirt upon their hook-like projections, and these become knotted and twisted by hard rubbing. If the fabric be too weak to be lifted up and down in the liquid bath, it may be laid on a sheet, over a folded blanket, and sponged on both sides with the soap or ammonia solution or with the naphtha. If the colors are changed a little by the alkalies, rinse the fabrics in vinegar or dilute acetic acid; if affected by acids, rinse in ammonia water.

Inflammable Materials. In the use of naphtha, benzine, turpentine, etc., great caution is necessary. The vapor of all these substances is extremely inflammable. They should never be used where there is *any* fire or light present, nor likely to be for several hours. A bottle containing one of them should never be left uncorked. Whenever possible, use them out-of-doors.

Prevention of Dirt. With both dust and grease, *prevention* is easier than removal. If the oily vapors of cooking and the volatile products of combustion be removed from the kitchen and cellar, and not allowed to dissipate themselves throughout the house, the greasy or smoky deposits will be prevented and the removal of the dust-particles and dust-plants will become a more mechanical process. Such vapors should be removed by special ventilators or by windows open at the top, before they become condensed and thus deposited upon everything in the house. Let in pure air, drive out the impure; fill the house with sunshine that it may be dry, and the problem of cleanness is largely solved.

CHAPTER III.

Stains, Spots, Tarnish.

Grease-spots.

Absorbents of Grease.

THESE three classes include the particular deposits resulting from accident, carelessness, or the action of special agents, as the tarnish on metals. They are numerous in character, occur on all kinds of materials and their removal is a problem which perplexes all women and which requires considerable knowledge and much patience to solve. A few suggestions may help some one who has not yet found the *best* way for herself.

Grease seems to be the most common cause of such spots. Small articles that can be laundered regularly with soap and water, give little trouble. These will be discussed in the following chapter.

Spots of grease on carpets, heavy materials, or colored fabrics of any kind which cannot be conveniently laundered, may be treated with absorbents. Heat will assist in the process by melting the grease. Fresh grease spots on such fabrics may often be removed most quickly by placing over the spot a piece of clean white blotting paper or butcher's wrapping paper, and pressing the spot with a warm iron. It is well to have absorbent paper or old cloth *under* the spot as well. Heat sometimes changes certain blues, greens and reds, so it is well to work cautiously and hold the iron a little above the goods till the effect can be noted.

French chalk,—a variety of talc, or magnesia, may be scraped upon the spot and allowed to remain for some time, or applied in fresh portions, repeatedly. If water can be used, chalk, fuller's earth or magnesia may be made into a paste with it or with benzine and this spread over the spot. When dry, brush the powder off with a soft brush.

For a fresh spot on fabrics of delicate texture or color, when blotting paper is not at hand, a visiting or other card may be split and the rough inner surface rubbed gently over the spot. Slight heat under the spot may hasten the absorption. Powdered soapstone, pumice, whiting, buckwheat flour, bran or any kind of coarse meal are good absorbents to use on carpets or upholstery. They should be applied as soon as the grease is spilled. Old spots will require a solvent and fresh ones may be treated in the same way.

Grease, as has been said, may be removed in three ways, by forming a solution, an emulsion, or a true soap. Wherever hot water and soap can be applied, the process is one of simple emulsion, and continued applications should remove both the grease and the entangled dust; but strong

Solvents of Grease.

soaps ruin some colors and textures. Ammonia or borax may replace the soap, still the water may affect the fabric, so the *solvents* of grease are safer for use. Chloroform, ether, alcohol, turpentine, benzine and naphtha, all dissolve grease. In their commercial state some of these often contain impurities which leave a residue, forming a dark ring, which is as objectionable as the original grease. Turpentine is useful for coarser fabrics, while chloroform, benzine and naphtha are best for silks and woolens. Ether or chloroform can usually be applied to all silks, however delicate. If pure, they are completely volatile and seldom affect colors. Whenever these solvents are used, it is well to place a circle of some absorbent material, like flour, crumbs of bread, blotting paper or chalk around the spot to take up the excess of liquid. Then rub the spot from the outside toward the center to prevent the spreading of the liquid, to thin the edges, and, thus, to ensure rapid and complete evaporation. The cleansing liquid should not be left to dry of itself. The cloth should be rubbed dry, but very carefully, for the rubbing may remove the nap from woolen goods and, therefore, change the color or appearance. Apply the solvent with a cloth as nearly like the fabric to be cleaned, in color and texture, as possible,

COOKING AND CLEANING.

or, in general, use a piece of sateen, which does not grow linty. A white cloth may be put under the stain to serve not only as an absorber of the grease and any excess of liquid, but also to show when the goods is clean. It is well to apply all cleansing liquids and all rubbing on the *wrong* side of the fabric. *None* of these solvents can be used near a flame.

The troublesome "dust spot" has usually a neglected grease spot for its foundation. After the grease is dissolved, the dust must be cleaned out by thorough rinsing with fresh liquid or by brushing after the spot is dry. <small>"Dust spots."</small>

Our grandmothers found ox-gall an efficient cleanser both for the general and special deposits. It is as effectual now as then and is especially good for carpets or heavy cloths. It may be used clear for spots, or in solution for general cleansing and brightening of colors. Its continued use for carpets does not fade the colors as ammonia or salt and water is apt to do. <small>Ox-gall.</small>

Cold or warm grease on finished wood can be wiped off easily with a woolen cloth moistened in *soapsuds* or with a few drops of turpentine. Soap should never be rubbed on the cloth except, possibly, for very bad spots round the kitchen stove or table. Solutions of washing soda, potash, or the friction, that may be used safely on unfin- <small>Grease-spots on Wood.</small>

ished woods, will take out the grease but will also destroy the polish.

Hot grease usually destroys the polish and sinks into the wood. It then needs to be treated like grease on unfinished wood or scraped out with fine steel wool or wire fibre, sandpaper or emery paper. The color and polish must then be renewed. When hot grease is spilled on wood or stone, if absorbents are not at hand, dash cold water on it immediately. This will solidify the grease and prevent its sinking deeply into the material.

Grease on Wall-paper or Leather.

Grease or oil stains on painted walls, wall-paper or leather, may be covered with a paste of pipe-clay, or French chalk and water. Let the paste dry and after some hours carefully brush off the powder. Sometimes a piece of blotting paper laid over the spot and a warm iron held against this, will draw out the grease. These pastes of absorbent materials are good for spots on marbles. They may then be mixed with turpentine or ammonia or soft soap.

Paint.

House paints consist mainly of oils and some colored earth. Spots of paint, then, must be treated with something which will take out the oil, leaving the insoluble coloring matter to be brushed off. When fresh, such spots may be treated with turpentine, benzine or naphtha. For delicate colors or textures, chloroform or naphtha is the safest. The turpentine, unless pure, may leave a resinous deposit. This may be dissolved in chloroform or benzine, but care should be exercised in the use of alcohol for it dissolves some coloring matters. Old paint spots often need to be softened by the application of grease or oil; then the old and the new may be removed together. Whenever practicable, let all spots soak a little, that the necessity of hard rubbing may be lessened.

Paint on stone, bricks or marble, may be treated with strong alkalies and scoured with pumice stone or fine sand.

Varnish and pitch are treated with the same solvents as paint—turpentine being the one in general use,—when the article stained will not bear strong alkalies. Pitch and tar usually need to be covered first with grease or oil, to soften them. *Varnish and Pitch.*

Wax spots made from candles should be removed by scraping off as much as possible, then treating the remainder with kerosene, benzine, ether, naphtha, or with blotting paper and a warm iron, as grease spots are treated. The soap and water of ordinary washing will remove slight spots. The spermaceti is often mixed with tallow which makes a grease spot, and with coloring matters which may require alcohol. *Wax.*

Food Stains.	Spots made by food substances are greasy, sugary or acid in their character, or a combination of these. That which takes out the grease will generally remove the substance united with it, as the blood in meat juices. The sugary deposits are usually soluble in warm water. If the acids from fresh fruits or fruit sauces affect the color of the fabric, a little ammonia water may neutralize the acid and bring back the color. Dilute alcohol may sometimes be used as a solvent for colored stains from fruit. Blood requires cold or tepid water, never hot. After the red color is removed soap and warm water may be used.

Blood stains on thick cloths may be absorbed by repeated applications of moist starch.

Wheel-grease and lubricants of like nature are mixtures of various oils and may contain soaps or graphite. The ordinary solvents of the vegetable or animal oils will remove these mixtures from colored fabrics by dissolving the oil. The undissolved coloring matter will, for the most part, pass through the fabric and may be collected on thick cloth or absorbent paper, which should always be placed underneath. From wash goods, it may be removed, readily, by strong alkalies and water, especially if softened first by kerosene or the addition of more grease, which increases the quantity of soap made. Graphite is the most difficult of removal.

COOKING AND CLEANING. 107

Ink spots are perhaps the worst that can be encountered, because of the great uncertainty of the composition of the inks of the present day. When the character of an enemy is known it is a comparatively simple matter to choose the weapons to be used against him, but an unknown enemy must be experimented upon, and conquest is uncertain. Methods adapted to the household are difficult to find, as the effective chemicals need to be applied with considerable knowledge of proportions and effects. Such chemicals are often poisons and, in general, their use by unskilled hands is not to be recommended.

Ink.

Fresh ink will sometimes yield to clear cold or tepid water. Skimmed milk is safe and often effective. If the cloth is left in till the milk sours, the result is at times more satisfactory. This has proved effective on light colored dress goods where strong acids might have affected the colored printed patterns. Some articles may have a bit of ice laid over the stain with blotting paper under it to absorb the ink solution. Remove the saturated portions quickly and continue the process till the stain has nearly or quite disappeared. The last slight stain may be taken out with soap and water. Some colored dress goods will bear the application of hot tartaric acid or of muriatic acid, a drop at a time, as on white goods.

Ink on carpets, table covers, draperies or heavy, dark cloths of any kind, may be treated immediately with absorbents to keep the ink from spreading. Bits of torn blotting paper may be held at the surface of the spot to draw away the ink on their hairy fibres. Cotton-batting acts in the same way. Meal, flour, starch, sawdust, baking soda or other absorbents may be thrown upon the ink and carefully brushed up when saturated. If much is spilled, it may be dipped up with a spoon or knife, adding a little water to replace that taken up, until the whole is washed out. Then dry the spot with blotting paper. The cut surface of a lemon may be used, taking away the stained portion as soon as blackened. Usually it requires hard rubbing to remove the last of the stain. Carpets may be rubbed with a floor brush, while a soft toothbrush may be used for more delicate articles. With white goods a solution of bleaching powder may be used, but there is always danger of rotting the fibres unless rinsing in ammonia water follow, in order that the strong acid of the powder may be neutralized.

Fresh ink stains on polished woods may be wiped off with clear water, and old stains of some inks likewise yield to water alone. The black coloring matter of other inks may be wiped off with the water, but a greenish stain may still remain which requires turpentine. In general, turpentine is the most effectual remover of ink from polished woods.

Indelible Inks. The indelible inks formerly owed their permanence to silver nitrate; now, many are made from aniline solutions and are scarcely affected by any chemicals. The silver nitrate inks, even after exposure to light and the heat of the sun or of a hot flat-iron, may be removed by bleaching liquor. The chlorine replaces the nitric acid forming a white silver chloride. This may be dissolved in strong ammonia or a solution of sodium hyposulphite. Sodium hyposulphite, which may be bought of the druggists, will usually remove the silver inks without the use of bleaching fluid and is not so harmful to the fibres. Some inks contain carbon which is not affected by any chemicals.

Aniline Inks. The aniline inks, if treated with chemicals may spread over the fabric and the last state be worse than the first. Other chemicals are effective with certain inks, but some are poisonous in themselves or in their products, some injure the fabric, and all require a knowledge of chemical reactions in order to be safely handled. Dried ink stains on silver, as the silver tops of inkstands may be moistened with chloride of lime and rubbed hard.

Marble. Polished marble may be treated with turpentine, "cooking soda" or strong alkalies, remembering that acids should never touch marble if it is desired to retain the polish. If the stain has penetrated through the polish, a paste of the alkali and turpentine may be left upon the spot for some time and then washed off with clear water.

Porcelain. Sometimes the porcelain linings of hoppers and bowls become discolored with yellowish-brown stains from the large quantities of iron in the water supply. These should be taken off with muriatic acid. Rinse in clean water and, lastly, with a solution of potash or soda to prevent any injurious action of the acid on the waste pipes.

Alcohol. Alcohol dissolves shellac. Most of the interior woodwork of the house, whether finish or furniture, has been coated with shellac in the process of polishing. If then, any liquid containing alcohol, as camphor, perfumes, or medicines, be spilled upon such woodwork and allowed to remain, a white spot will be made, or if rubbed while wet, the dissolved shellac will be taken off and the bare wood exposed.

Heat. Heat also turns varnish and shellac white. A hot dish on the polished table leaves its mark. These white spots should be rubbed with oil till the color is restored.

If a little alcohol be brushed over the spot with a feather, a little of the surrounding shellac is dissolved and spread over the stained spot. Hard rubbing with kerosene will, usually, remove the spot and renew the polish. If the shellac be removed and the wood exposed the process of renewal must be the original one of coloring, shellacing and polishing, until the necessary polish is obtained.

Caustic alkalies, strong solutions of sal-soda, potash and the like, will eat off the finish. Apply sweet, olive, or other vegetable oils, in case of such accidents. The continued use of oils or alkalies always darkens natural woods. *Alkalies.*

The special deposits on metals are caused by the oxygen and moisture of the air, by the presence of other gases in the house, or by acids or corroding liquids. Such deposits come under the general head of tarnish. *Chemical Compounds.*

The metals, or their compounds, in common use are silver, copper and brass, iron and steel, tin, zinc and nickel. Aluminum is rapidly taking a prominent place in the manufacture of household utensils.

There is little trouble with the general greasy film or with the special deposits on articles in daily use, if they are washed in hot water and soap, rinsed well and wiped dry each time. Yet certain articles of food act upon the metal of tableware and cooking utensils, forming true chemical salts. The salts of silver are usually dark colored and in- *Tarnish on Silver.*

soluble in water or in any alkaline liquid which will not also dissolve the silver. Whether found in the products of combustion, in food, as eggs, in the paper or cloth used for wrapping, in the rubber band of a fruit jar, or the rubber elastic which may be near the silver, sulphur forms with silver a grayish black compound—a sulphide of silver. All the silver sulphides are insoluble in water. Rub such tarnished articles, before washing, with common salt. By replacement, silver chloride, a white chemical salt, is formed, which is soluble in ammonia. If the article be not washed in ammonia it will soon turn dark again. Most of these metallic compounds formed on household utensils being insoluble, friction must be resorted to.

Silverware.

The matron of fifty years ago took care of her silver herself or closely superintended its cleaning, for the articles were either precious heirlooms or the valued gifts of friends. The silver of which they were made was hardened by a certain proportion of copper and took a polish of great brilliancy and permanence. The matron of to-day, who has the same kind of silver or who takes the same care, is the exception. *Plated* ware is found in most households. The silver deposited from the battery is only a thin coating of the pure soft metal—very bright when new, but easily scratched, easily tarnished, and never again capable of taking a beautiful polish. The utensils, being of comparatively little value, are left to the table-girl to clean. She, naturally, uses the material which will save her labor.

In order to ascertain if there was any foundation for the prevalent opinion that there was mercury or some equally dangerous chemical in the silver powders commonly sold, samples were purchased in Boston and vicinity, and in New York and vicinity. *Silver Powders*

Of the thirty-eight different kinds examined in 1878

  25 were dry powder.
  10 " partly liquid.
  3 " soaps.

Of the twenty-five powders, fifteen were chalk or precipitated calcium carbonate, with a little coloring matter, usually rouge.

  6 were diatomaceous earth.
  2 " fine sand entirely.
  2 " fine sand partly.

Mercury was found in none. No other injurious chemical was found in any save the "electro-plating battery in a bottle," which contained potassium cyanide, KCN, a deadly poison; but it was labeled poison, although the label also stated that "all salts of silver are poison when taken internally." This preparation does contain silver, and does deposit a thin coating, but it is not a safe article for use.

Silver Polishes.

Of the nine polishes, partly liquid, five contained alcohol and ammonia for the liquid portion; four, alcohol and sassafras extract. The solid portion, in all cases, was chalk, with, in one case, the addition of a little jeweler's rouge.

The caution to be observed in the use of these preparations is in regard to the fineness of the material. A few coarse grains will scratch the coating of soft silver. Precipitated chalk, $CaCO_3$, or well-washed diatomaceous earth, SiO_2, seem to be of the most uniform fineness.

Whiting.

We may learn a lesson in this, as well as in many other things, from the old-fashioned housewife. She bought a pound of whiting for twelve cents, sifted it through fine cloth, or floated off the finer portion, and obtained twelve ounces of the same material, for three ounces of which the modern matron pays twenty-five or fifty cents, according to the name on the box.

The whiting may be made into a paste with ammonia or alcohol, the article coated with this and left till the liquid has evaporated. Then the powder should be rubbed off with soft tissue paper or soft unbleached cloth, and polished with chamois.

Cleaning of Silver in Quantity.

Sometimes it is desirable to clean a large quantity of silverware at one time, but the labor of scouring and polishing each piece is considerable. They may all be placed carefully in a large kettle—a clean

COOKING AND CLEANING. 115

wash-boiler is convenient for packing the large pieces—and covered with a strong solution of washing-soda, potash or borax. Boil them in this for an hour or less. Let them stand in the liquor till it is cold; then polish each piece with a little whiting and chamois. A good-sized piece of zinc boiled with the silverware will help to clean away any sulphides present, by replacing the silver in them and forming a white compound.

Silver should never be rubbed with nor wrapped in woolen, flannel or bleached cloth of any kind, for sulphur is commonly used in bleaching processes; nor should rubber in any form be present where silver is kept. The unused silver may be wrapped in soft, blue-white or pink tissue paper, prepared without sulphur, and packed in unbleached cotton flannel cases, each piece separately. *Protection of Silverware.*

Silver jewelry, where strong soap or other alkali is not sufficient for the cleaning process, may be immersed in a paste of whiting and ammonia, and when dry, brushed carefully with a soft brush. If there be a doubt as to the purity of the silver, replace the ammonia by sweet oil or alcohol. The ammonia and whiting are also good for gold. Jewelry cleaned with water may be dried in boxwood sawdust. *Silver Jewelry.*

Care is necessary in the use of ammonia in or on "silver" topped articles, as vinaigrettes. These tops *Copper and Silver.*

THE CHEMISTRY OF

Brass, Copper.

are often made of copper with a thin layer of silver. Whenever the ammonia remains upon the copper, it dissolves it, forming poisonous copper salts.

Brass and copper must not be cleaned with ammonia unless due care is taken that every spot be rinsed and wiped perfectly dry. Nothing is better for these metals than the rotten-stone and oil of old-time practice. These may be mixed into a paste at the time of cleaning or be kept on hand in quantity. Most of the brass polishes sold in the market are composed of these two materials, with a little alcohol or turpentine or soap, to form an emulsion with the oil. Oxalic acid may be used to clean these metals, but it must be rinsed or rubbed off completely, or green salts will be formed. Copper or brass articles cleaned with acids tarnish much more quickly from the action of moisture in the air than when cleaned with the oil and soft powder. Small spots may be removed with a bit of lemon juice and hot water. An occasional rubbing with kerosene helps to keep all copper articles clean and bright. Indeed, kerosene is useful on any metal, as well as on wood or glass.

Oxidation of Metals.

The presence of water always favors chemical change. Therefore iron and steel rapidly oxidize in damp air or in the presence of moisture. All metallic articles may be protected from such action by a thin oily coating. Iron and steel articles not in use may be covered with a thin layer of vaseline.

COOKING AND CLEANING. 117

Rust spots may be scoured off with emery and oil covered with kerosene or sweet oil for some time and then rubbed hard, or in obstinate cases, touched with muriatic acid and then with ammonia, to neutralize the acid. *Iron-rust.*

A stove rubbed daily with a soft cloth and a few drops of kerosene or sweet oil may be kept black and clean, though not polished. Substances spilled on such a stove may be cleaned off with soap and water better than on one kept black with graphite. *Care of Stoves.*

Nickel is now used in stove ornaments, in the bathroom, and in table utensils. It does not oxidize or tarnish in the air or with common use. It can be kept bright by washing in hot soap-suds and rinsing in very hot water. It may be rubbed with a paste of whiting and lard, tallow, alcohol or ammonia. *Nickel.*

Aluminum does not tarnish readily, and may be rubbed with the whiting or with any of the fine materials used for silver. A paste is prepared by the dealers for this special use. *Aluminum.*

Kitchen utensils, with careful use, may be kept clean by soap and water or a liberal use of ammonia. Fine sand-soap must occasionally be used when substances are burned on or where the tin comes in contact with flame. Kerosene is a good cleaner for the zinc stove-boards; vinegar and water, if there is careful rinsing afterward, or a strong solution of salt and water may be used. *Kitchen Utensils.*

CHAPTER IV.

LAUNDRY.

THE health of the family depends largely upon the cleansing operations which belong to the laundry. Here, too, more largely perhaps than in any other line of cleaning, will a knowledge of chemical properties and reactions lead to economy of time, strength and material.

The numerous stains and spots on table linen and white clothes are dealt with in the laundry, and, also, all fabrics soiled by contact with the body.

Body clothes, bed linen and towels become soiled not only by the sweat and oily secretions of the body, but also with the dead organic matter continually thrown off from its surface. Thus the cleansing of such articles means the removal of stains of varied character, grease and dust, and all traces of organic matter.

The two most important agents in this purification are water and soap.

Water. Pure water is a chemical compound of two gases, hydrogen and oxygen (H_2O). It has great solvent and absorbent power, so that in nature pure water is never found, though that which falls

COOKING AND CLEANING.

in sparsely-settled districts, at the end of a long storm, may be approximately pure. The first fall of any shower is mixed with impurities which have been washed from the air. Among these may be acids, ammonia and carbon in the form of soot and creosote. It is these impurities which cause the almost indelible stain left when rain-water stands upon window-sills or other finished wood.

Rain-water absorbs more or less carbon dioxide from various sources and, soaking into the soil, often comes in contact with lime, magnesia and other compounds. Water saturated with carbon dioxide will dissolve these substances, forming carbonates or other salts which are soluble, and such water is known as "hard."

Hard and Soft Water. Water for domestic uses is called either "hard" or "soft" according as it contains a greater or less quantity of these soluble salts. When soap—a chemical compound—is added to hard water, it is decomposed by the water; and the new compound formed by the union of the lime with the fatty acid of the soap is insoluble and is deposited upon the surface of any articles with which it comes in contact. Therefore, large quantities of soap must be used before there can be any action upon the dirt. It has been estimated that each grain of carbonate of lime per gallon causes an increased expenditure of two ounces of soap per 100 gallons, and that the increased expense for soap in a household of five persons where such hard water is used, might amount to five or ten dollars yearly.*

Temporary and Permanent Hardness. When the hardness is caused by calcium carbonate it is called "temporary" hardness, because it may be overcome by boiling. The excess of carbon dioxide is driven off and the lime precipitated. The same precipitation is brought about by the addition of sal-soda or ammonia. When the hardness is due to the sulphates of lime and magnesia, it cannot be removed by boiling or by the addition of an alkali; it is then known as "permanent."

Public water supplies are often softened before delivery to the consumers by the addition of slaked lime, which absorbs the carbon dioxide and the previously dissolved carbonate is precipitated. If this softening process be followed by filtration, the number of bacteria will be lessened, and the water, thereby, rendered still purer.

All water for use with soap should, then, be naturally soft or made soft by boiling or by the addition of alkalies, ammonia or sal-soda.

Soap. Another important material used in the laundry is soap. "Whether the extended use of soap be preceded or succeeded by an improvement in any community—whether it be the precursor or the re-

---

* Water Supply, William P. Mason, p. 366.

COOKING AND CLEANING. 121

sult of a higher degree of refinement among the nations of the earth—the remark of Liebig must be acknowledged to be true, that the quantity of soap consumed by a nation would be no inaccurate measure whereby to estimate its wealth and civilization. Of two countries with an equal amount of population, the wealthiest and most highly civilized will consume the greatest weight of soap. This consumption does not subserve sensual gratification, nor depend upon fashion, but upon the feeling of the beauty, comfort and welfare attendant upon cleanliness; and a regard to this feeling is coincident with wealth and civilization."*

Many primitive people find a substitute for soap in the roots, bark or fruit of certain plants. Nearly every country is known to produce such vegetable soaps, the quality which they possess of forming an emulsion with oily substances being due to a peculiar vegetable substance, known as Saponin. Many of these saponaceous barks, roots and fruits are now used with good results—the "soap bark" of the druggist being one of the best substances for cleansing dress goods, especially black, whether of silk or wool.

Soap Substitutes.

The fruit of the soapberry tree—*Papindus Saponaria*—a native of the West Indies, is said to

* Muspratt's Chemistry as Applied to *Arts and Manufactures*.

be capable of cleansing as much linen as sixty times its weight of soap.

Wood ashes were probably used as cleansing material long before soap was made, as well as long after its general use. Their properties and value will be considered later.

Composition of Soaps.

Soaps for laundry use are chiefly composed of alkaline bases, combined with fatty acids. Their action is "gently but efficiently to dispose the greasy dirt of the clothes and oily exudations of the skin to miscibility with, and solubility in wash water."*

Oily matters, as we have seen, are soluble in certain substances, as salt is soluble in water, and can be recovered in their original form from such solutions by simple evaporation. Others in contact with alkalies, form emulsions in which the suspended fatty globules make the liquid opaque, as in soapsuds. The soap is decomposed by water, the alkali set free acts upon the oily matter on the clothes, and unites with it, forming a new soap. The freed fatty acid remains in the water, causing the "milkiness," or is deposited upon the clothes.

"Potash" and "Soda."

Certain compounds of two of the alkali metals, potassium and sodium, are capable of thus saponifying fats and forming the complex substances known as soaps. For the compounds of these al-

*Chemistry applied to the Manufacture of Soaps and Candles.—Morfit.

COOKING AND CLEANING. 123

kalies employed in the manufacture of soap, we shall use the popular terms "potash" and "soda," as less likely to cause confusion in our readers' minds. Potash makes soft soap; soda makes hard soap. Potash is derived from wood ashes, and in the days of our grandmothers soft soap was the universal detergent. Potash (often called pearlash) was cheap and abundant. The wood fires of every household furnished a waste product ready for its extraction. Aërated pearlash (potassium bicarbonate), under the name of saleratus, was used for bread. Soda-ash was, at that time, obtained from the ashes of seaweed, and, of course, was not common inland.

The discovery by the French manufacturer, Leblanc, of a process of making soda-ash from the cheap and abundant sodium chloride, or common salt, has quite reversed the conditions of the use of the two alkalies. Potash is now about eight cents a pound, soda-ash is only three.

In 1824, Mr. James Muspratt, of Liverpool, first carried out the Leblanc process on a large scale, and he is said to have been compelled to give away soda by the ton to the soap-boilers, before he could convince them that it was better than the ashes of kelp, which they were using on a small scale. The soap trade, as we now know it, came into existence after the soap-makers realized the

Manufacture of Soda-ash.

value of the new process. Soda-ash is now the cheapest form of alkali, and housekeepers will do well to remember this fact when they are tempted to buy some new "——ine" or "Crystal."

In regard to the best form in which to use the alkali for washing purposes, experience is the best guide,—that is, experience reinforced by judgment; for the number of soaps and soap substitutes in the market is so great, and the names so little indicative of their value, that only general information can be given.

In the purchase of soap, it is safest to choose the make of some well-known and long-established firm, of which there are several who have a reputation to lose, if their products are not good; and, for an additional agent, stronger than soap, it is better to buy sal-soda or soda-ash (sodium carbonate) and use it knowingly, than to trust to the highly-lauded packages of the grocery.

The Use of Washing Soda.

Washing soda should never be used in the solid form, but should be dissolved in a separate vessel, and the solution used with judgment. The injudicious use of the solid is probably the cause of the disfavor with which it is often regarded. One of the most highly recommended of the scores of "washing compounds" formerly in the market, doubtless owed its popularity to the following directions: "Put the contents of the box into one

COOKING AND CLEANING. 125

quart of boiling water, stir well, and add three quarts of cold water; this will make one gallon. For washing clothes, allow two cupfuls of liquid to a large tub of water."

As the package contained about a pound of *washing soda*, this rule, which good housekeepers have found so safe, means about two ounces to a large tub of water, added before the clothes are put in.

Ten pounds of washing soda can be purchased of the grocer for the price of this one-pound package with its high-sounding name. Nearly all the compounds in the market depend upon washing soda for their efficiency. Usually they contain nothing else. Sometimes soap is present and, rarely, borax. In one or two, a compound of ammonia has been found.

Ammonia may be used with soap or as its substitute. The ammonia ordinarily used in the household is an impure article and its continued use yellows bleached fabrics. The pure ammonia may be bought of druggists or of dealers in chemical supplies and diluted with two or even four parts of water. Borax, where the alkali is in a milder form than it is in washing soda, is an effectual cleanser, disinfectant and bleacher. It is more expensive than soda or ammonia, but for delicate fabrics and for many colored articles it is the safest alkali in use.

<small>Ammonia</small>

Turpentine also is valuable in removing grease. A tablespoonful to a quart of warm water is a satisfactory way of washing silks and other delicate materials. It should never be used in hot water, for much would be lost by evaporation, and in this form it is more readily absorbed by the skin, causing irritation and discomfort.

PREPARATION FOR GENERAL WASHING.

White goods are liable to stains from a variety of sources. Many of these substances when acted upon by the moisture of the air, by dust, or alkalies, change their character, becoming more or less indelible; colorless matters acquire color and liquids become semi-solid. All such spots and stains should be taken out before the clothes are put into the general wash to be treated with soap.

Fruit stains are the most frequent and possibly the most indelible, when neglected. These should be treated when fresh.

The juices of most fruits contain sugar in solution, and *pectose*, a mucilaginous substance which will form jelly. All such gummy, saccharine matters are dissolved most readily by boiling water, as are mucilage, gelatine and the like. To remove them when old, an acid, or in some cases, a bleaching liquid, like "chloride of lime" solution or Javelle water will be needed.

COOKING AND CLEANING.   127

Stretch the stained part over an earthen dish and pour *boiling* water upon the stain until it disappears. How to use the acid and the Javelle water will be explained later on.

Wine stains should be immediately covered with a thick layer of salt. Boiling milk is often used for taking out wine and fruit stains.

Most fruit stains, especially those of berries, are bleached readily by the fumes of burning sulphur. SO_2. These fumes are irritating to the mucous membrane and care should, therefore, be taken not to inhale them. Stand by an open window and turn the head away. Make a cone of stiff paper or cardboard or devote a small tin tunnel to this purpose. Cut off the base of the paper cone, leaving it level and have a small opening at the apex. On an old plate or saucer, place a small piece of sulphur, set it on fire, place over it the cone or tunnel, and hold the moistened stain over the chimney-like opening. Have a woolen cloth handy to put out the sulphur flame if the piece is larger than is needed. A burning match sometimes furnishes enough SO_2 for small spots. Do not get the burning sulphur on the skin. *Use of Sulphur Fumes*

Medicine stains usually yield to alcohol. Iodine dissolves more quickly in ether or chloroform. *Medicine.*

Coffee, tea and cocoa stain badly, the latter, if neglected, resisting even to the destruction of the *Tea, Coffee, Cocoa.*

fabric. These all contain tannin, besides various coloring matters. These coloring matters are "fixed" by soap and hot water. Clear boiling water will often remove fresh coffee and tea stains, although it is safer to sprinkle the stain with borax and soak in cold water first. (A dredging box filled with borax is a great convenience in the laundry.) Old cocoa and tea stains may resist the borax. Extreme cases require extreme treatment. Place on such stains a small piece of washing-soda or "potash." Tie it in and boil the cloth for half an hour. It has already been said that these strong alkalies in their solid form cannot be allowed to touch the fabrics without injury. With this method, then, there must be a choice between the stain and an injury to the fabric.

An alkaline solution of great use and convenience is Javelle water. It will remove stains and is a general bleacher. This is composed of one pound of sal-soda with one-quarter pound of "chloride of lime" — *calcium hypochlorite* — in two quarts of boiling water. Let the substances dissolve as much as they will and the solution cool and settle. Pour off the clear liquid and bottle it for use. Be careful not to let any of the solid portion pass into the bottle. Use the dregs to scour unpainted woodwork, or to cleanse waste pipes.

When a spot is found on a white table-cloth,

place under it an overturned plate. Apply Javelle water with a soft tooth-brush. (The use of a brush protects the skin and nails.) Rub gently till the stain disappears, then rinse in clear water and finally in ammonia. "Chloride of lime" always contains a powerful acid, as well as some free chlorine.

Blood stains require clear, cold or tepid water, for hot water and soap render the red coloring matter less soluble. When the stain is brown and nearly gone, soap and hot water may be used. Blood.

Meat juice on the table linen is usually combined with more or less fat. This also yields most readily to the cold water, followed by soap.

Stains made by mucus should be washed in ammonia before soap is added. When blood is mixed with mucus, as in the case of handkerchiefs, it is well to soak the stains for some hours in a solution of salt and cold water—two tablespoonfuls to a quart. Double the quantity of salt for heavier or more badly stained articles. The salt has a disinfecting quality, and its use in this way is a wise precaution in cases of catarrh.

Milk exposed to the air becomes cheesy, and hot water with milk makes a substance difficult of solution. Milk stains, therefore, should be washed out when fresh and in cold water. Milk.

Grass stains dissolve in alcohol. If applied im- Grass.

mediately, ammonia and water will sometimes wash them out. In some cases the following methods have proved successful, and their simplicity recommends them for trial in cases where colors might be affected by alcohol. Molasses, or a paste of soap and cooking soda, may be spread over the stain and left for some hours, or the stain may be kept moist in the sunshine until the green color has changed to brown, then it will wash out in clear water.

Mildew causes a spot of a totally different character from any we have considered. It is a true mold, and like all plants requires warmth and moisture for its growth. When this necessary moisture is furnished by any cloth in a warm place, the mildew grows upon the fibres. During the first stages of its growth, the mold may be removed, but in time it destroys the fibres.

Strong soapsuds, a layer of soft soap and pulverized chalk, or one of chalk and salt, are all effective if, in addition, the moistened cloth be subjected to strong sunlight, which kills the plant and bleaches the fibres. Bleaching powder or Javelle water may be tried in cases of advanced growth, but success cannot be assured.

Some of the animal and vegetable oils may be taken out by soap and cold water or dissolved in naphtha, chloroform, ether, etc.

COOKING AND CLEANING. 131

Some of the vegetable oils are only sparingly soluble in cold, but readily soluble in hot alcohol. The boiling point of alcohol is so low that care should be taken that the temperature be not raised to the ignition point.

Mineral oil stains are not soluble in any alkaline or acid solutions. Kerosene will evaporate in time. Vaseline stains should be soaked in kerosene before water and soap touch them.

Ink spots on white goods are the same in character as on colored fabrics. Many of the present inks are made from aniline or allied substances instead of the iron compounds of the past. Aniline black is indelible; the colored anilines may be dissolved in alcohol. Where the ink is an iron compound the stain may be treated with oxalic, muriatic or hot tartaric acids, applied in the same manner as for iron-rust stains. No definite rule can be given, for some inks are affected by strong alkalies, others by acids, while some will dissolve in clear water.

Ink.

The present dyes are so much more stable than those of twenty-five years ago, that pure lemon juice or a weak acid like hydrochloric, has no effect upon many colors. Any acid should, however, be applied with caution. If the color is affected by acids, it may often be restored by dilute ammonia.

The red iron-rust spots *must* be treated with acid. These are the result of true oxidation—the union

Red Iron-rust.

of the oxygen of the air with the iron in the presence of moisture. The salt formed is deposited upon the fabric which furnishes the moisture. Ordinary "tin" utensils are made from iron coated with tin, which soon wears off, so no moist fabric should be left long in tin unless the surface is entire.

Iron-rust is, then, an oxide of iron. The oxides of iron, copper, tin, etc., are insoluble. The chlorides, however, are soluble. Replace the oxygen with the chlorine of hydrochloric acid and the iron compound will be dissolved. The method of applying the acid is very simple.

Fill an earthen dish two thirds full of hot water and stretch the stained cloth over this. Have near two other dishes with clear water in one and ammonia water in the other. The steam from the hot water will furnish the heat and moisture favorable for chemical action. Drop a little hydrochloric (muriatic) acid, HCl, on the stain with a medicine dropper. Let it act a moment, then lower the cloth into the clear water. Repeat till the stain disappears. Rinse carefully in the clear water and, finally, immerse in the ammonia water that any excess of acid may be neutralized and the fabric protected.

Salt and lemon juice are often sufficient for a slight stain, probably because a little hydrochloric acid is formed from their union.

Many spots appear upon white goods which resemble those made by iron-rust, or the fabrics themselves acquire a general yellowish tinge. This is the result of the use of bluing and soap, where there has been imperfect rinsing of the clothes. The old-time bluing was pure indigo. This is insoluble, but, by its use, a fine blue powder was spread among the fibres of the cloth. It required careful manipulation, which it usually had. Indigo with sulphuric acid can be made to yield a soluble paste. This is the best form of bluing which can be used, for a very little gives a dark, clear blue to water, and overcomes the yellowish tinge which cotton or linen will acquire in time unless well bleached by sunshine. The expense and difficulty of obtaining this soluble indigo has led to the substitution of numerous solid and liquid "blues" by the use of which the laundress is promised success with little labor. Most of these liquid bluings contain some iron compound. This, when in contact with a strong alkali, is broken up and the iron is precipitated. If, then, bluing be used where all the soap or alkali has not been rinsed from the clothes, this decomposition and precipitation takes place, and a deposit of iron oxide is left on the cloth. This must be dissolved by acid like any iron-rust.

Some "blues" are compounds of ultramarine, a brilliant blue silicate of aluminum. These are gen-

Bluing.

erally used in the form of a powder which is insoluble, settles quickly and, thereby, leaves blue spots or streaks. It is very difficult to prevent these when insoluble powdered "blues" are used. This silicate combined with hydrochloric acid forms a jelly-like mass from which a white precipitate is formed. These ultramarine blues are sometimes recommended because of this white precipitate, obviating, as is said, the yellowish results of careless rinsing, inevitable when iron "blues" are used. The advice is misleading, for no precipitate is formed unless an acid be added.

When solid bluing is used it should be placed in a flannel bag and stirred about in a basin of hot water. In this way only the finest of the powder is obtained. After this blued water is poured into the tub, it must be continually stirred, to prevent the powder from settling in spots or streaks upon the clothes.

Bleaching.

First, then, the removal of all dirt, and second, the removal, by thorough rinsing, of all soap or other alkalies used in the first process, and third, long exposure to air and sunshine should render the use of bluing unnecessary. The experience of many shows that clothes that have never been blued, never need bluing. In cities where conveniences for drying and bleaching in the sunshine are few, and where clear water or clear air are often un-

COOKING AND CLEANING.

attainable, a thorough bleaching two or three times a year is a necessity; but in the country it is wiser to abolish all use of bluing and let the great bleacher, the sun, in its action with moisture and the oxygen of the air, keep the clothes white as well as pure.

Freezing aids in bleaching, for it retains the moisture, upon which the sun can act so much the longer. The easiest household method of bleaching where clean grass, dew and sunshine are not available, is by the use of "bleaching powder." In the presence of water and weak acids, even carbonic acid, oxygen and chlorine are both set free from the compound. At the moment of liberation the action is very powerful. The organic coloring matters present are seized upon and destroyed, thereby bleaching the fabric.

Directions for the use of the powder usually accompany the can in which it is bought. The woman who knows that the acid always present in the powder must be completely rinsed out or neutralized by an alkali, may use her bleaching powder with safety and satisfaction.

All special deposits should be removed before the general cleansing of the fabric is undertaken. Grease and other organic matters are the undesirable substances which are to be disposed of in the general cleansing. Grease alone is more quickly acted upon by hot water than by cold, but other

General Cleansing.

organic matter is fixed by the hot water. Therefore, while hot water melts the grease quickly, the mixture may be thus spread over the surface and may not be removed by the soap.

Soaking.

An effective method, proved by many housewives of long experience, is to soap thoroughly the dirtiest portions of the clothes, fold these together toward the center, roll the whole tightly, and soak in cold water. The water should just cover the articles. In this way the soap is kept where it is most needed, and not washed away before it has done its work. When the clothes are unrolled the dirt may be washed out with less rubbing.

Too long soaking when a strong soap is used, which has much free alkali, would weaken the fabric. Judgment, trained by experience must guide in such cases, so that effective cleaning depends upon careful manipulation.

Boiling.

Whether to boil or not to boil the clothes depends largely upon the purity of the materials used and the degree of care exercised. Many persons feel that the additional disinfection which boiling ensures is an element of cleanness not to be disregarded; others think it unnecessary under ordinary conditions, while others insist that boiling *yellows* the clothes.

"Yellowness."

The causes of this yellowness seem to be:

COOKING AND CLEANING.

Impure materials in the soap used;

The deposition, after a time, of iron from the water or the boiler;

The imperfect washing of the clothes—that is, the organic matter is not thoroughly removed.

The safest process seems to be to put the clothes into cold water with little or no soap, let the temperature rise gradually to the boiling point and remain there a few minutes.

Soap is more readily dissolved by hot water than by cold, hence the boiling should help in the complete removal of the soap and may well precede the rinsing.

Borax—A tablespoonful to every gallon of water—added to each boilerful serves as a bleacher and an aid in disinfection. The addition of the borax to the last rinsing water is preferred by many. In this case, the clothes should be hung out quite wet, so that the bleaching may be thorough.

"Scalding," or the pouring of boiling water over the clothes is not so effectual for their disinfection as boiling, because the temperature is so quickly lowered. *Scalding.*

The main points in laundry cleansing seem to be:— *Necessities for Good Cleansing.*

The removal of all stains;

Soft water and a good quality of soap;

The use of strong alkalies in solution only;

Not too *hot* nor too *much* water while the soap is acting upon the dirt;

Thorough rinsing, that all alkali may be removed;

Long exposure to sunlight—the great bleacher and disinfectant.

Structure of Fibres. The fibres of cotton, silk and wool vary greatly in their structure, and a knowledge of this structure, as shown under the microscope, may guide to proper methods of treatment.

Cotton The fibres of cotton, though tubular, become much flattened during the process of manufacture, and under the microscope show a characteristic twist, with the ends gradually tapering to a point. It is this twist which makes them capable of being made into a firm, hard thread.

Wool. The wool fibre, like human hair, is marked by transverse divisions, and these divisions are serrated. These teeth become curled, knotted or tangled together by rubbing, by very hot water, or by strong alkalies. This causes the shrinking which should be prevented. When the two fibres are mixed there is less opportunity for the little teeth to become entangled and, therefore, there is less shrinkage.

Linen. Linen fabrics are much like cotton, with slight notches or joints along the walls. These notches serve to hold the fibres closely together and enable them to be felted to form paper. Linen, then, will shrink, though not so much as wool, for the fibres are more wiry and the teeth much shorter.

Silk fibres are perfectly smooth, and when rubbed, simply slide over each other. This produces a slight shrinkage in the width of woven fabrics. *Silk.*

All wool goods, then, require the greatest care in washing. The different waters used should be of the same temperature, and never too hot to be borne comfortably by the hand. *Washing of Woolens.*

The soap used should be in the form of a thin soap solution. No soap should be rubbed on the fabric, and only a good *white* soap, free from rosin, or a soft potash soap, is allowable. Make each water slightly soapy and leave a *very* little in the fabric at the end, to furnish a dressing as nearly like the original as possible.

Many persons prefer ammonia or borax in place of the soap. For pure white flannel, borax gives the best satisfaction, on account of its bleaching quality. Whatever alkali is chosen, care should be exercised in the quantity taken. Only enough should be used to make the water very soft.

The fibres of wool collect much dust upon their tooth-like projections, and this should be thoroughly brushed or shaken off before the fabric is put into the water. All friction should be by squeezing, not by rubbing. Wool should not be wrung by hand. Either run the fabric smoothly through a wringer or squeeze the water out, that the fibres may not be twisted. Wool may be well dried by rolling the article tightly in a thick dry towel or sheet and squeezing the whole till all moisture is absorbed. Wool should not be allowed to freeze, for the teeth will become knotted and hard.

Linen, like wool, collects much dirt upon the surface which does not penetrate the fabric. Shake this off and rub the cloth as little as possible. Linen or woolen articles should not be twisted in the drying process, as it is sometimes impossible to straighten the fibres afterward.

Setting of Colors.

Colored cottons should have their colors fixed before washing. Salt will set most colors, but the process must be repeated at each washing. Alum sets the colors permanently, and at the same time renders the fabric less combustible, if used in strong solution after the final rinsing.

Very Dirty Articles.

Dish cloths and dish towels must be kept clean as a matter of health, as well as a necessity for clean, bright tableware. The greasy dish cloth furnishes a most favorable field for the growth of germs. It must be washed with soap and hot water and dried thoroughly each time. All such cloths should also form a part of the weekly

COOKING AND CLEANING. 141

wash and be subjected to all the disinfection possible, with soap, hot water and long drying in sunshine and the open air. Beware of the disease-breeding, greasy and damp dish cloth hung in a warm, dark place!

Oven towels, soiled with soot and crock, may be soaked over night, or for some hours, in just kerosene enough to cover, then washed in cold water and soap.

With very dirty clothes or for spots, where hard rubbing is necessary, much strength may be saved by using a scrubbing brush.

Laundry tubs should be carefully washed and dried. Wooden tubs, if kept in a very dry place, and turned upside down, may have the bottoms covered with a little water. *Care of Laundry Furniture.*

The rubber rollers of the wringer may be kept white by rubbing them with a clean cloth and a few drops of kerosene.

All waste and overflow pipes, from that of the kitchen sink to that of the refrigerator, become foul with grease, lint, dust, and other organic matters that are the result of bacterial action. They are sources of contamination to the air of the entire house and to the food supply, thereby endangering health. All bath, set-bowl and water closet pipes should be flushed generously once a day, at least, the kitchen sink pipe with clear boiling *Care of Plumbing.*

water; and once a week all pipes should have a thorough cleaning with a strong boiling solution of washing-soda and a monthly flushing with caustic potash. The plumbers recommend the "stone" or crude potash for the kitchen pipe. This is against their own interests, for many a plumber's bill is saved where the housewife knows the danger and the means of prevention of a grease-coated sink drain. The pipe of the refrigerator should be cleared throughout its entire length with the soda solution. Avoid any injury to the metallic rims of the waste pipes by using a large tunnel.

Old-fashioned styles of overflow pipes retain a large amount of filth, and it is very difficult to dislodge it. A common syringe may be devoted to this purpose. By its patient, frequent use even this tortuous pipe may be kept clean.

Ideal Cleanness.

Sanitary Cleanness.   Ideal cleanness requires the cleanness of the individual, of his possessions, and of his environment. Each individual is directly responsible for his personal cleanness and that of his possessions; but over a large part of his environment he has only indirect control. Not until direct personal responsibility is felt in its fullest sense, and exercised in all directions toward the formation and carrying out of sufficient public laws, will sanitary

COOKING AND CLEANING. 143

cleanness supplant the *cure* of a large number of diseases by their *prevention*.

Many of the diseases of childhood are directly traceable to uncleanness, *somewhere*. By these diseases the system is often so weakened that others of different character are caused which, though slow in action, may baffle all science in their cure.

The necessity of forming systematic *habits* of cleanness in the young is the first step toward sanitary health. They should, then, step by step, as they are able to grasp the *reasons* for the habits, be educated in all the sciences which give them the knowledge of the cause and effects of uncleanness, the methods of prevention and removal, and the relation of all these to building laws and municipal regulations.

<small>Personal Cleanness.</small>

The first environment to be kept clean is the home. But personal cleanness and household cleanness should not be rendered partially futile by unclean schoolhouses, public buildings and streets.

<small>School-house Sanitation.</small>

The *housekeeping* of the schoolhouses, especially, should be carried on with a high regard to all hygienic details, since here the degree of danger is even greater than in the home. In public schoolhouses the conditions favorable to the presence of disease germs abound. If present, their growth is rapid, and the extent of contagion beyond calculation. The coöperation of all most interested—pupils and teachers—should be expected and required as firmly as their coöperation in any other department of education.

The sanitary condition of every school building should be a model object lesson for the home; then, instruction in personal cleanness will carry the weight of an acknowledged necessity.

Schoolhouses which are models of sanitary cleanness will cause a demand for streets and public conveyances of like character; then *all* public buildings will be brought under the same laws of evident wisdom.

Not till the *right* of cleanness is added to the *right* to be well fed, and both are assured to each individual by the knowledge and consent of the whole people, can the greater gospel of prevention make good its claims.

CHAPTER V.

THE HOUSEKEEPER'S LABORATORY
OR
THE CHEMICALS FOR HOUSEHOLD USE.

THE thrifty housewife may not only save many dollars by restoring tarnished furniture and stained fabrics, but may also keep her belongings fresh and "as good as new," by the judicious use of a few chemical substances always ready at her hand.

It is essential, however, that she know their properties and the effect they are likely to have on the materials to be treated, lest more harm than good result from their use. A good example is the instant disappearance of all red iron-rust stains when treated with a drop of hydrochloric acid (the muriatic acid of the druggist). If, however, the acid is not completely washed out, the fabric will become eaten, and holes will appear, which, in the housekeeper's eye, are worse than the stains. This danger may be entirely removed by adding ammonia to the final rinsing water, which neutralizes any remaining acid, and the stained tray-cloth or sheet is perfectly whitened.

The chemicals for household use are chiefly

acids, alkalies, and solvents for grease. Acids and alkalies are opposed to each other in their properties, and if too much of either has been used, it may be rendered innocent, or neutralized by the other; as, when soda has turned black silk brown, acetic acid or vinegar will bring the color back.

The acids which should be on the chemical shelf of the household are acetic, hydrochloric (muriatic), oxalic, tartaric. Vinegar can be used in many cases instead of acetic acid; but vinegar contains coloring matters which stain delicate fabrics, and it is better to use the purified acid, especially as the so-called vinegar may contain sulphuric acid.

Some bright blue flannels and other fabrics, when washed with soap or ammonia become changed or faded in color. If acetic acid or vinegar be added to the last rinsing water, the original appearance *may* be restored. Not all shades of blue are made by the same compounds, hence not all faded blues can be thus restored.

The use of these acids has been indicated in the previous pages, and there remains to be considered, only certain cautions. Hydrochloric acid is volatile. It will escape even around a glass stopper and will eat a cork stopper; therefore, either the glass stopper should be tied in with an impervious cover—rubber or parchment—or a rubber stopper used, for the escaping fumes will rust metals and eat fabrics.

Oxalic acid should be labeled *poison*.

The bleaching agents, "chloride of lime," calcium hypochlorite, sodium hypochlorite, sodium hyposulphite (thiosulphite), owe their beneficent effect to substances of an acid nature which are liberated from them, and the clothes should be rinsed in a dilute alkali to neutralize this effect. They should all be used in solution only, and should be kept in bottles with rubber stoppers.

Sulphurous acid gas (SO_2), obtained by burning sulphur, is also a well-known agent for bleaching. It will often remove spots which nothing else will touch. The amount given off from a burning sulphur match will often be sufficient to remove from the fingers fruit stains or those made by black kid gloves.

The alkalies which are indispensable are:

1st. Ammonia,—better that of the druggist than the often impure and always weak "household ammonia." The strong ammonia is best diluted about one half, since it is very volatile, and much escapes into the air.

2d. Potash, which is found at the grocers in small cans. — The lye obtained from wood ashes owes its caustic and soap-making properties to this substance. Potash is corrosive in its action, and must be used with discretion.

Crystallized sodium carbonate, the sal-soda of the grocer, is not, chemically speaking, an alkali, but it gives all the effect of one, since the carbonic acid readily gives place to other substances.

Sal-soda is a very cheap chemical, since it is readily manufactured in large quantities, and forms the basis of most of the washing powders on the market. With grease, it forms a soap which is dissolved and carried away.

3d. Borax is a compound of sodium with boric acid, and acts as a mild alkali. It is the safest of all the alkalies, and affects colored fabrics less than does ammonia.

Solvents for grease are alcohol, chloroform, ether, benzine, naphtha, gasolene—all volatile—kerosene and turpentine. Of these chloroform is the most costly, and is used chiefly for taking spots from delicate silks. Fabrics and colors not injured by water may be treated by alcohol or ether. Benzine, naphtha or gasolene are often sold, each under the name of the other. If care is taken to prevent the spreading of the ring, they can be safely used on any fabric. They do not mix with water, and are very inflammable.

The less volatile solvents are kerosene and turpentine. Kerosene is a valuable agent in the household, and since some of the dealers have provided a deodorized quality, it should find an even wider

COOKING AND CLEANING. 149

use. The lighter variety is better than the 150-degree fire test, which is the safe oil for lamps. As has been indicated in the preceding pages, the housewife will find many uses for this common substance.

On account of the purity and cheapness of kerosene, turpentine is less used than formerly, although it has its advantages.

These household chemicals should have their own chest or closet, as separate from other bottles as is the medicine chest, and especially should they be separate from *it*. Many distressing accidents have occurred from swallowing ammonia by mistake.

In addition to these substances, certain others may be kept on hand, if the housewife has sufficient chemical knowledge to enable her to detect adulteration in the groceries and other materials which she buys.

A few of these simple tests are given with the chemicals needed.

Directions for Using the Housekeeper's Laboratory.

When directed to make a solution acid or alkaline, always test it by means of the litmus paper:—

Blue turned to red means *acid*. Red turned to blue means *alkaline*.

Only by following the directions can the test be relied upon. Under other circumstances than those given, the results may mean something else.

Use the *acids* in glass or china vessels only. Metals may be attacked. Do not touch brass with ammonia.

To test for *sulphuric acid* or soluble *sulphate* in soda, cream of tartar, baking powder, vinegar, sugar or syrup: Add muriatic acid (HCl) to the solution (if the insoluble part is sulphate of lime, it will dissolve in HCl on heating), then add barium chloride ($BaCl_2$). A heavy white precipitate proves the presence of sulphuric acid, either free or combined. If the solution is not distinctly acid at first, it is not free.

To test for *lime* in cream of tartar, baking powder, sugar or syrup: Make the solution alkaline with ammonia and ammonium oxalate. A fine white precipitate proves presence of lime. Good cream of tartar will dissolve in boiling water, and will show only slight cloudiness when the test for lime is applied.

To test for *phosphates* in cream of tartar or baking powder: Make acid by nitric acid (HNO_3), and add ammonium molybdate. A fine yellow precipitate or yellow color proves presence of phosphates.

To test for *chlorides* in soda, baking powder,

COOKING AND CLEANING. 151

sugar, syrup or water: Make the solution (a fresh portion) acid with nitric acid (HNO_3), and add silver nitrate ($AgNO_3$). A white, curdy precipitate or a cloudiness indicates chlorides.

To test for *ammonia* in baking powder: Add a small lump of caustic potash to a strong water solution. Red litmus will turn blue in the steam, on heating.

To test for *alum* in cream of tartar, baking powder or bread: Prepare a fresh decoction of logwood; add a few drops of this to the solution or substance, and render acid by means of acetic acid ($C_2H_4O_2$). A yellow color in the acid solution proves absence of alum. A bluish or purplish red, more or less decided, means more or less alum.

If the label of a washing powder claims it to be something new, and requires that it be used without soda, as soda injures the clothes, it can be tested as follows: Put half a teaspoonful of the powder into a tumbler, add a little water, then a few drops of muriatic acid. A brisk effervescence will prove it to be a carbonate, and if the edge of the tumbler is held near the colorless flame of an alcohol lamp, the characteristic yellow color of sodium will appear and complete the proof. If the acid is added, drop by drop, until no more effervescence occurs, and there remains a greasy scum on the surface of the liquid in the tumbler, the compound contains soap as well as sal-soda, for the acid unites with the alkali of the soap and sets free the grease.

If some very costly silver polishing powder is offered as superior to all other powders, a drop or two of muriatic acid will decide whether or not it is chalk or whiting, ($CaCO_3$) by the effervescence or liberation of the carbonic acid gas.

CAUTION! Use a new solution or a fresh portion of the first one for each new test. This it is essential to remember.

To judge of the *quantity* of any of the substances, it is necessary to have a *standard* article with which to compare the *suspected* one. Take the same quantity of each, and subject each to the same tests. A very correct judgment may thus be formed. Besides this laboratory there should be in every household an emergency case, placed in an accessible and well-known cupboard, but out of the reach of children. It should be plainly labeled and kept stocked with the various solutions, plasters, ointments, etc., with which the house-mother soothes wounded nerves as well as bruiséd noses.

BOOKS OF REFERENCE.

CONSULTED IN THE REVISION OF THE CHEMISTRY OF COOKING AND CLEANING.

Foods: Composition and Analysis..........A. W. Blyth
Dietetic Value of Bread.............John Goodfellow
Food, Manuals of Health............Albert J. Bernays
Food and Its Functions................James Knight
Analysis and Adulteration of Foods........James Bell
Food ....A. H. Church
Foods and Feeding..............Sir Henry Thompson
The Chemistry of Cookery........W. Mattieu Williams
Chemistry of Wheat, Flour and Bread and Technology of Bread Making..............Wm. Jago
The Spirit of Cookery.............J. L. W. Thudichum
Food in Health and Disease............I. Burney Yeo
Diet in Sickness and Health...........Mrs. Ernest Hart
Chemistry and Economy of Food, U. S. Dept. Agriculture, Bulletin 21, 1895......W. O. Atwater
Also Bulletins 28, 29, 31, 35, 37.
Farmers' Bulletins 34, 42.
Dietetics ....Gilman Thompson
Practical, Sanitary and Economic Cooking.......
Mrs. Mary Hinman Abel
How to Feed Children.............Louise E. Hogan
The Science of Nutrition.............Edward Atkinson
Food Materials and Their Adulterations.........
Ellen H. Richards

BOOKS OF REFERENCE.

Handbook of Invalid Cooking..........Mary A. Boland
The Young Housekeeper................Maria Parloa
Chemie der menschlichen Nahrungs und Genus-
    mittel ....J. Koenig
Physiological Chemistry of the Animal Body.....
                                  Arthur Gamgee
A Text-book of Physiological Chemistry...Hammarsten
Chemistry of Daily Life...................Lassar Cohn
Organic Chemistry............................. Remsen
Inorganic Chemistry .... Remsen
Dust and Its Dangers.............T. Mitchell Prudden
The Story of the Bacteria.........T. Mitchell Prudden
The Story of Germ Life............Prof. H. W. Conn
Home Sanitation..Ellen H. Richards and Marion Talbot
Household Economics..........Mrs. Helen Campbell
How to Drain a House................George Waring
Homes and All About Them............E. C. Gardner
The House that Jill Built...............E. C. Gardner
From Attic to Cellar.................Mrs. Eliz. F. Holt
The Art of Laundry Work..........Florence R. Jack
The Micro-Organisms of Fermentation...........
                                 Alfred Jörgensen
Our Secret Friends and Foes.........Percy Frankland
Housework and Domestic Economy....M. E. Haddon
Emergencies and How to Meet Them......J. W. Howe
Manual of Lessons on Domestic Economy....H. Major
Handbook of Sanitary Information..............
                                Roger S. Tracy, M. D.
The Food Products of the World...Dr. Mary E. Green
Le Pain et la Panification.............Leon Boutroux
Eating and Drinking............Albert H. Hoy, M. D.
Text-Book of Am. Physiology......Prof. Wm. Howell

INDEX.

Absorbents of grease, 100, 101
Acids, 16, 17, 21, 41, 146
  Acetic, 38
  Butyric, 35
  for iron stains, 132
  Mineral, 21.
  Muriatic or Hydrochloric, 13, 17, 19, 41, 132, 146
  Oxalic, 116, 147
  Stearic, 43
  Tannic, 50
Air, a substance, 85
  as food, 67
  not the agent of change, 73
  pollution of, 84
  pure, 83
Albumin, 49
Albuminoids, 50
Alcohol, 30, 36
Alcohol, as solvent, 102, 110, 148
  product of fermentation, 30, 36, 38
Alkalies, caustic, 89, 111
  Volatile, 89
Alkali metals, 88
Aluminum, 117
Ammonia, 89
  uses of, 73, 93, 102, 125, 139, 147
Ammonium, 88, 89
Animal body, a living machine, 47
  repair of, 48
Art of cooking, 56, 62
Atoms, 5, 11
Atomic weight, 10, 11
  of hydrogen, 14

Bacteria, 36, 39, 74, 76, 77, 81
  action of in disease, 80
  as flavor producers, 62
  food of, 81
  spores of, 75
Bacteriology of bread-making, 36
Baking powder, 23
Beans, 52, 64
Beer, 29
Benzine, 98, 102, 148
Biscuits, 39

Bleaching, 134, 135
Bleaching powder, 135 (See chloride of lime and Javelle Water)
Blinds, 82
Blood-stains, 106, 129
Blotting paper for ink, 108
Bluing, 133, 134
Books for reference, 153
Borax, 125, 128, 137, 139, 148
Brass, 116
Bread-making, chemical reactions in 29, 30, 36
Bread, as food, 33
  crust, 39
  fermented, 36
  flavor in, 39
  ideal, 34
  home made, 37
  leavened, 35
  object of baking, 38
  reason for kneading,
  temperature of baking, 37, 38, 39, 54,
    of fermentation, 37
  stale, 39
Butter, 43
Butyric acid, 35
cream of tartar, 41, 42

Caesium, 88
Calcium hypochlorite, 128
Calories, 47
Cane sugar, 28, 29
Carbohydrates, 26, 44, 63
Carbon dioxide (carbonic acid gas), 16, 17, 18, 19, 20, 25, 30, 36, 37
  method of obtaining, 40
Casein, 52
Caustic alkalies, 89
Cayenne pepper, 59
Cellulose, 27
Cheesecloth for cleaning, 93
Chemical arithmetic, 18, 21
Chemical change, 3, 10, 28
  produces heat, 25
Chemical elements, tables of, 15, 16, 17

INDEX.

Chemical elements, laws of combination, 19
  equations, 18, 21
Chemical Laws, 10, 13
Chemical reaction, 21, 25
  reactions in bread and beer making, 36
Chemical Symbols, 11
Chemicals for household use, 145
Chloride of lime, 126, 127, 128, 129, 147
Chlorine, 13
Chloroform, 102, 148
Cleaning of brass, 116
  fabrics, 97, 98
  glass, 96
  paint, 93
  silver, 111, 116
  wood, 90, 91, 92, 93
  powders, 113
  problems of, 90
  processes of, 88, 90
Cleanness, ideal and sanitary, 142
  of school houses, 144
  personal, 143
  philosophy of, 82, 85
  public, 144
Cocoa and coffee stains, 127, 128
Collagen, 50
Colors, setting of, 140, 146
Combustion of food, 25, 26
  products of, 84
Condiments, 56, 58, 59
Consumption, 83
Conversion of starch, 28, 30
Cooking, American, 58
  art of, 56, 57, 62
  chemistry of, 58
  discretion in, 62
  economy in, 60
  effect of, 54
  fats, 46
  nitrogenous food, 50, 53
  object of, 53
  starch, 32
  vegetables, 60
Copper, 115, 116
Cottonseed oil, 43
Cream of tartar, 23, 41, 42

Decomposition, 64
Definite proportions, laws of, 19
Development of flavor, 56
Dextrose, 29
Diatase, 29
Diet, 63, 65

Diet, fat in, 45
Dietaries, 68, 69
Digestion, 28, 61, 63, 66
  of fats, 44
  is solution, 28
Dirt, definition of, 78
  prevention of, 98
Disease, cause of, 80
  prevention of, 79
Dish cloths and towels, 140
Dust, 71, 72, 73, 75, 87, 88
  composed of, 77
  germs, 80
  in air, 72, 76
  meteoric, 73
  on fabrics, 97, 98
  on wood, 92
  spots, 103

Economy in cooking, 60
  of mixed diet, 65
Effect of cooking, 54
  of condiments, 58
Eggs, 51
Elements, Chemical, 9
Energy, sources of, 44
  mechanical unit of, 47
Ether, 102, 148
Exchange value, 14, 15, 17, 20
Expansion of gases, 6
  of water, 40

Fabrics, 97, 98
Fat, effect of high temperature on, 46
  digestion of, 44
  in diet, 44
Fats, 24, 43, 45, 55, 88
Fermentation, 35, 39
Finish of woods, 90
Flavor, 46, 56, 57, 58, 60
Flour, use of in bread, 39
Food, office of, 24, 69
  water and air as, 68
Forces causing change, 4
Fruit stains, 126, 127
Fuel in body, 47
Fungi, 74

Gases, 3
Gasolene, 148
Germs, 74, 80, 81
Glass, 96
Glucose, 29
Gluten, 52
Grass stains, 129
Grease, 87, 88, 100, 101, 102, 104, 135

INDEX.

Grease, on wood, 103
  solvents for, 91
Groups of elements, 20
Growth, nitrogenous food required for, 48
Gums, 24

Heat produced by chemical change, 24
  source of in animals, 25
Housekeeper's laboratory, directions for using, 149-152
Hydrochloric acid, (see muriatic)
Hydrogen, 9, 27, 44

Ideal bread, 34
Indigo, 133
Inflammable substances, 98
Ink indelible, 109
  stains, 107, 108, 131
Inoculation, 82
Iron rust, removal of, 117, 131, 132, 145

Javelle Water, 126, 127, 128, 129, 130
Jewelry, 115

Kerosene, 91, 92, 96, 111, 116, 117, 131, 141, 148, 149
Kitchen utensils, 117

Laboratory, housekeeper's, 149
Lard, 43
Laundry, 118-142
Law of Combination, 13
  definite proportion, 19
  multiple proportion, 19
Leather, 94
Leaven, 35
Legumin, 52
Lentils, 65
Levulose, 29
Lithium, 88, 89

Marble, 95, 109
Matter, changes in, 1, 2, 3, 4
  definition of, 1
  forms of, 3
  states of, 5
Medicine stains, 127
Metals, 95, 111, 116
Mildew, 130
Milk stains, 129
Mineral acids, 21
Mixed diet, 65
Molds, 74, 77, 79

Molecular weight, 11
Molecules, 5, 6, 11
Mucous stains, 129
Muriatic acid, 41

Naphtha, 148
Nature's scavengers, 78
Nickel, 117
Nitrogen, 48
Nitrogenous food, 47, 49, 68
  cooking of, 50, 55

Oils, 43, 45, 88, 92
Oil finish, 91
Oil Stains, 130
Olive Oil, 44, 45
Oxalic acid, 147
Ox-gall, 103
Oxygen, 9, 26, 43
Oysters, 51

Paint, 93, 104
Paper, 94
Pastry, 54
Pathogenic germs, 81
Pearlash,
Pepsin, 64
Peptones, 64
Physical change, 2, 3
Pitch, 105
Plated silver ware, 112
  cyanide, 113
Plumbing, care of, 141
Porcelain, 96, 110
Potash, 103, 122, 123, 147
Potassium, 88
Preparation for food, of starch, sugar and fat, 24
Prevention, 80, 98
Principles of diet,
Products of decomposition, 64
Proportion of nitrogenous food required, 68
Pumice, 95

Rations, 69
Reference books, 153
Removal of dust, spots and stains, 87
Restoring color, 97
Rubidium, 88
Rust of iron, 117

Saliva, 63
Sal-soda, 148
Salt, 7, 41, 42
School house sanitation, 143

INDEX.

Seasonable diet, 65
Serving, 62
Shellac, dissolved by alcohol, 111
Silver, cleaning of, 111, 113, 114, 115
  nitrate,
  polish, 113, 114
Silver-ware, 112, 115
Soap, 89, 120, 122, 124, 137, 139
  bark, 121
  berry tree, 121
Soda, 7, 42, 122, 124
Soda ash, 17, 123, 124
Sodium, 87
Sodium carbonate, 148
Solution, 6, 7, 28, 50, 81
Solvents, 78, 91, 101, 102, 106, 148
Source of energy, 44
Spores, 75
Spots, 100, 118
Stains, 100, 106, 118, 126, 127, 128
Starch, 24, 27, 28, 29, 30, 31
  cooking of 32, 55, 61
Stearic acid, 43
Stimulants, 60
Stoves, care of, 117
Sugar, 2, 24, 27, 29
  cane, 28
  fruit, 28
  milk, 27, 28
Suet, 43
Sulphur fumes, 127, 147

Sunlight, 82, 83, 84, 85
Symbols, 11, 12,
Syrups, 7

Tables, 15, 16, 17, 21, 23
Tannin, 128
Tarnish, 100, 101
Tea stains, 127, 128
Temperature, 26, 46, 49, 52, 53
Turpentine, 91, 102, 103, 126, 148

Ultramarine, 133, 134
Unit of value, 14
Utensils, Kitchen, 117

Valence, 14
Varnish, 91, 105
Vegetables, 60

Wall paper, 94
Washing-Soda, 124, 125
Water, 18, 118, 119, 120
  as food, 67
  hard, 119, 120
Wax, 91, 105
Whiting, 114
Wine stains, 121
Wood finish, 90, 91, 92
Woolens, washing of, 139

Yeast, 33, 35, 36, 37, 38, 74, 78

www.ingramcontent.com/pod-product-compliance
Lightning Source LLC
Chambersburg PA
CBHW031455160426
43195CB00010BB/992